HOME IMPROVEMENT LIBRARY™

Flooring Projects & Techniques

MINNETONKA, MINNESOTA

Contents

5900 Green Oak Drive
Minnetonka, Minnesota 55343
1-800-328-3895

Printed in U.S.A.

Books available in this series:
Everyday Home Repairs, Decorating With Paint & Wallcovering, Carpentry: Tools • Shelves • Walls • Doors, Building Decks, Kitchen Remodeling, Home Plumbing Projects & Repairs, Basic Wiring & Electrical Repairs, Workshop Tips & Techniques, Advanced Home Wiring, Carpentry: Remodeling, Landscape Design & Construction, Bathroom Remodeling, Built-in Projects for the Home, Kitchen & Bathroom Ideas, Refinishing & Finishing Wood, Exterior Home Repairs, Home Masonry Repairs & Projects, Building Porches & Patios, Deck & Landscape Ideas, Flooring Projects & Techniques, Advanced Deck Building, Advanced Home Plumbing

Library of Congress
Cataloging-in-Publication Data

Flooring projects & techniques.

p. cm.—(Black & Decker home improvement library)
Includes index.
ISBN 0-86573-678-2 (hardcover).
ISBN 0-86573-679-0 (softcover).
1. Floors. 2. Floor coverings.
I. Cy DeCosse Incorporated.
II. Series.
TH2521.F633 1996
690'.16—dc20 96-26990

President: Iain Macfarlane

Created by: The Editors of Creative Publishing, international, Inc., in cooperation with Black & Decker. BLACK&DECKER is a trademark of the Black & Decker Corporation and is used under license.

Group Executive Editor: Paul Currie
Managing Editor: Kristen Olson
Project Managers: Ron Bygness, Lori Holmberg
Editorial Director: Mark Johanson
Associate Creative Director: Tim Himsel
Senior Editor: Bryan Trandem
Lead Editor & Researcher: Joel Schmarje
Editors: David Mahoney, Jon Simpson
Editorial Assistant: Andrew Sweet
Copy Editor: Janice Cauley
Lead Art Director: John Hermansen
Art Directors: Geoff Kinsey, Gina Seeling
Technical Production Editors: Dan Cary, Gary Sandin
Vice President of Photography & Production: Jim Bindas

Shop Supervisor: Phil Juntti
Lead Set Builder: Rob Johnstone
Set Builders: Troy Johnson, John Nadeau
Production Staff: Tom Hoops, Jeanette Moss, Christopher Ostrom, Mike Schauer, Herb Schnabel, Brent Thomas, Greg Wallace, Kay Wethern
Creative Photo Coordinator: Cathleen Shannon
Studio Manager: Marcia Chambers
Lead Photographer: Charles Nields
Photographers: Rebecca Schmitt, Greg Wallace
Contributing Photography: AlliedSignal Fibers, Dalton, GA; American Olean; Armstrong World Industries; Bruce Hardwood Floors; Color Tile, Inc.; Congoleum Corp.; DuPont Approved *Stainmaster®* Carpet; Florida Tile Industries, Inc.; Heritage Custom Kitchens; Mannington Resilient Floors; Trade Commission of Spain

Technical Consultants: Ahrendt Carpet Co., Minneapolis, MN—Charles Selander; Resilient Floor Covering Institute—Walter Anderson
Contributing Manufacturers: Dal-Gard™ crack/isolation membrane; Dallas Specialty and Manufacturing Company; Rubble Tile Distributors, Minnetonka, MN; Stone Mountain Carpet Mill Outlet, St. Louis Park, MN

Printed on American paper by:
R.R. Donnelley & Sons Co.
10 9 8 7 6 5

Introduction

Of all home improvement projects, installing new flooring offers perhaps some of the greatest rewards for the time and money you invest. Properly installed, a new floor is one of the longest-lasting improvements you can make, and one you can enjoy and appreciate whenever you step through the door.

The wide variety of floor coverings available today makes planning a new floor an exciting, though challenging, prospect. *Flooring Projects & Techniques* will help you sort through all the options and select the flooring that best satisfies your needs. Resilient flooring, tile, hardwood, and carpet are each covered in detail.

To start the selection process, browse through the gallery of flooring ideas, take notes, and read the design tips. Keep this information in mind when selecting flooring. Next, you'll learn how to estimate and purchase the necessary materials and plan your work.

Before you begin installing your new floor, some preparation is required. This book devotes an entire section to the crucial preparation process. You will learn how to evaluate your existing floor, how to remove various types of flooring, and how to repair or prepare the subfloor. You will also learn how to install new underlayment to ensure that your flooring installation will be both durable and attractive.

At the heart of the book are detailed, step-by-step instructions for installing floor coverings, including resilient vinyl sheets and tile, ceramic tile and natural stone, and hardwood. New flooring products developed in recent years make do-it-yourself projects easier than ever. Within each of the basic flooring categories you will find installation options to match your skill level and your budget.

Carpet, one of the most popular and versatile of all floor coverings, gets full treatment in this book. We show you techniques for using specialty tools to achieve professional-looking results, and lead you step-by-step through an installation, from installing tackless strips to making the final cuts.

Before you begin a project, read through all the steps carefully to gain a complete understanding of the process. Also, consult the "Everything You Need" lists at the beginning of each project to determine which tools and materials are necessary.

Resilient sheet vinyl is a practical and attractive choice for kitchen floors. It is moisture-resistant and easy to clean, and its flexible, cushioned surface reduces dish breakage and makes standing during kitchen chores less fatiguing. Sheet vinyl comes in a range of styles, often mimicking the look of slate tiles (above) and other popular flooring materials. Sheet vinyl also can be custom-cut to create original designs, as shown in the sun room on the opposite page.

A Gallery of Flooring Ideas

Flooring is an integral element of any interior design. When choosing a flooring style, always consider how it will interact with the other design elements in your home. Look at home magazines and flooring product catalogs to help you visualize how different floorings can affect the look of a room.

There are also practical considerations when choosing a floor covering. Flooring should be well suited to the needs of a room. For example, in a kitchen where food spills are common, sheet vinyl is a more practical choice than expensive, deep-pile wool carpet.

The photos on these pages show some of the ways that practical flooring choices can contribute to interior design.

Resilient tiles can create an effect much like sheet vinyl, but are easier for the do-it-yourselfer to install. Usually 12 × 12" in size, resilient tiles are durable and easy to clean. They make attractive and practical floors in entryways (right) and kitchens (below).

Contrasting resilient tiles can be arranged in a checkerboard pattern or in other geometric designs. This foyer floor (right) was created by alternating vinyl tiles of different colors. It simulates the look of marble at a fraction of the cost.

Marble tile is an expensive, top-quality flooring material well suited for formal settings, like the neo-Roman living room and dining room shown above. Here, the hallway was separated and defined by the use of darker, contrasting tiles.

Ceramic tile is a common choice for small rooms, like the bathroom shown above, but it also works well in simple contemporary designs, as in the kitchen shown below.

Hardwood parquet floors use tiles that incorporate wood pieces of different sizes and shades. Parquet floor tiles can be used to create intricate patterns (above) or simple designs (below).

Hardwood flooring is available both in narrow strips and wide planks. The random-plank floor shown above combines different-size boards to make a simple pattern that complements any room style. Hardwood makes a perfect neutral background that does not compete with the ornate elements of a room.

Wall-to-wall carpet adds color and warmth to a room, while complementing other design elements. In the country-style room shown above, the blue carpet echoes colors found in the furniture upholstery, and a stair runner cut from the same carpet makes a graceful transition to the upper floor. In the room shown at left, loop-pile carpet creates an earthy, textured effect.

Dense plush carpet creates a feeling of relaxation that is right at home in private quarters, like this bedroom (right).

Thick loop-pile carpet (above) can make a room quiet, warm, and comfortable.

Low-pile carpet (right), is very versatile and will adopt the style and feel of the other room elements that surround it. In this parlor, it takes on a formal look.

Compare flooring samples, available from flooring distributors, to see which looks best with your room colors and furnishings. If you plan to repaint walls, use color chips to pick colors that will complement your new floor.

Planning Your New Floor

Because floors are highly visible, appearance is perhaps the most important consideration when choosing flooring. Start your search by browsing through magazines and visiting flooring retail stores.

Of course, there are other characteristics to keep in mind when choosing a floor covering. Cost and ease of installation are key concerns for most people. For others, how the flooring feels underfoot is important. In a room subject to moisture, heavy traffic, or other special conditions, consider how different floor coverings perform in these situations. See the comparisons on pages 18 to 19 for help in selecting a floor covering that fits your needs.

When estimating materials for your project, add 5 to 10% to your total to allow for waste caused by trimming. (For some carpet installations, you will need to add even more.) After your project is completed, save any extra flooring material in case repairs are required.

This section shows:

Tips for Planning a Flooring Project

Establish a work sequence that makes sense. Many flooring projects are done as part of a more comprehensive remodeling project. In this case, the flooring should be installed after the walls and ceiling are finished, but before the fixtures are put in. Protect new flooring with heavy paper or tarps when completing your remodeling project.

Measure the area of the project room to calculate how much material you will need. Measure the full width and length of the space to determine the overall square footage, then subtract the square footage of areas that will not be covered, such as stairways, cabinets, and other permanent fixtures.

CHECKLIST FOR PLANNING A FLOORING PROJECT

Read the following sections, and use this checklist to organize your activities as you start your flooring project.

❏ Measure the project area carefully. Be sure to include all nooks and closets, as well as areas under all movable appliances. Calculate the total square footage of the project area.

❏ Use your measurements to create a floor plan on graph paper.

❏ Sketch pattern options on tracing paper laid over the floor plan to help visualize what the flooring will look like when it is installed.

❏ Identify areas where the type of floor covering will switch, and choose the best threshold material to use for the transition.

❏ Estimate the amount of preparation materials needed, including underlayment sheets and floor leveler.

❏ Estimate the amount of installation materials needed, including the floor covering and other supplies, such as adhesives, grouts, thresholds, tackless strips, and screws. For help in estimating, go to a building supply center and read the labels of materials and adhesives to determine coverage.

❏ Make a list of the tools needed for the job. Locate sources for tools you will need to buy or rent.

❏ Estimate the total cost of the project, including all preparation materials, flooring and installation materials, and tools. For expensive materials, comparison-shop to get the best prices.

❏ Check with building supply centers or flooring retail stores for delivery cost. Delivery service is often inexpensive and well worth the additional charge.

❏ Determine how much demolition you will need to do, and plan for debris removal, either through your regular garbage collector or a dumpster-rental company.

❏ Plan for the temporary placement of furnishings and removable appliances to minimize disruption of your daily routine.

Comparing Floor Coverings

RESILIENT FLOORING

Description: A flexible flooring product made primarily of vinyl, resilient flooring is often colored and patterned to simulate the look of ceramic or natural-stone tile. Resilient flooring material ranges in thickness from 1/16" to ⅛". It is usually glued to an underlayment. In some cases, the entire project area is covered with adhesive (called "full-spread"); in other installations, only the edges of the material are glued down (called "perimeter bond").

Uses: Resilient flooring is a versatile surface that can be used almost anywhere, though it is most often found in kitchens and bathrooms.

Types: Available in sheets or tiles. Sheet vinyl comes in 6-ft.-wide or 12-ft.-wide rolls, with either a felt backing for full-spread installation or a PVC backing for perimeter-bond installations. Resilient tiles typically come in 12" squares, and often have self-adhesive backing for easy installation.

Cost: Sheet vinyl is priced per square yard; tile, per square foot. Resilient vinyl flooring typically costs about the same as carpet and is less expensive than ceramic tile or hardwood. Prices for resilient flooring depend on several factors, including the percentage of vinyl in the material, the overall thickness of the product, and the complexity of the pattern.

Preparation: Because resilient flooring reveals underlying flaws, the underlayment must be very smooth. The amount of preparation needed varies, depending on the condition of the existing underlayment.

Installation: Resilient flooring is generally easier to install than other floor coverings. Self-adhesive tile is the easiest type to install; full-spread sheet vinyl is slightly more difficult. For tile installations, establishing accurate layout lines is essential. For sheet vinyl, making an accurate template of the room perimeter is critical.

CERAMIC TILE

Description: Ceramic tile is a hard, durable material that comes in a wide variety of colors, patterns, shapes, and sizes. Thicknesses range from 3/16" to ¾". Traditional ceramic tiles are made from oven-baked clay. Natural-stone tiles are cut from quarried stone.

Uses: This durable, all-purpose flooring material is an excellent choice for high-traffic areas. Ceramic tile is commonly installed in bathrooms, entryways, and kitchens.

Types: Common types include unglazed quarry tile, glazed ceramic tile, and porcelain mosaic tile. Natural-stone tiles include marble, slate, and granite.

Cost: In general, these materials are more expensive than other floor coverings. Natural-stone flooring is usually more costly than ceramic tile.

Preparation: Preparing for a ceramic tile installation can be a more expensive and time-consuming process than for other types of flooring, especially if cementboard underlayment is used to provide a stable and water-resistant foundation. Underlayment must be perfectly flat and level, and the layout must be planned and executed very carefully.

Installation: Ceramic tile is more time-consuming to install than other types of flooring. Installation requires patient work to make sure the tiles are square to the layout lines, evenly spaced, and bonded securely. Cutting tiles requires special tools and techniques. Joints between tiles are filled with tile grout and sealed to ensure durability.

HARDWOOD

Description: Hardwood is a rigid, durable flooring material. It is available in solid or laminated planks, and in laminated parquet squares. Most hardwood flooring has tongue-and-groove construction to enhance bonding between pieces.

Uses: Hardwood floors give a warm and elegant look to any room and are sturdy enough to hold up well in high-traffic areas. Hardwood floors are particularly popular in dining rooms, living rooms, and entryways.

Types: Traditional solid-wood planks are the most common type of hardwood used in flooring, but the growing selection of plywood-backed and synthetic-laminate products is well suited for do-it-yourselfers. Oak and maple are the most common wood species available, and size options include narrow strips, wide planks, and parquet squares.

Cost: In general, installing a hardwood floor is slightly less expensive than installing a ceramic tile floor. Prices for hardwood flooring products vary, but laminated products are typically less costly than solid hardwood. Availability of solid-wood flooring is decreasing, driving prices up.

Preparation: Hardwood floors require relatively little preparation, since they need no underlayment and can be installed directly over a subfloor. They can even be laid over resilient flooring, if it is in good condition.

Installation: Do-it-yourself installation of laminated hardwood products is fairly easy. Most products are either glued down or "floated" on a foam cushion; parquet squares with self-adhesive backs are installed much like self-adhesive vinyl tiles. Solid hardwood planks must be nailed down; a job best left to professionals.

CARPET

Description: Carpet is a soft, flexible floor covering made of synthetic or natural fibers bonded to a mesh backing and usually sold in 12-ft.-wide rolls. It is most commonly available in solid colors, although many patterns are also available.

Uses: Carpet is a popular choice for bedrooms, family rooms, and hallways. It is chosen primarily for comfort, rather than durability, although new, improved materials are increasingly resistant to wear.

Types: The two basic types of carpeting are loop-pile, which uses uncut loops of yarn to create a textured look and feel, and cut-pile, which has trimmed fibers that give a more uniform appearance.The two pile types can be combined in one carpet. Some types of carpet come with a cushioned backing already attached and are designed for easy glue-down installation.

Cost: Carpet is similar in price to resilient flooring, though prices vary greatly, depending on density and fiber material. For example, wool carpet costs considerably more than most synthetic-fiber carpet.

Preparation: Preparation is a relatively simple matter of installing tackless strips and padding. Preparation for installing a cushion-back carpet is even easier, since this product is simply glued down to underlayment without pads and tackless strips.

Installation: Although not difficult, installing carpet requires some special tools and techniques. A roll of carpet can be quite heavy, requiring two people to move and position it.

Design continuity can be provided by using the same flooring in adjacent rooms. The entryway and hallway shown above are joined by square ceramic tiles and border tiles laid in a ruglike pattern.

Design Tips for Flooring

No matter what type of floor you are installing, choose your colors, patterns, and textures carefully, since it is likely you will be living with your selection for many years—or even decades. Flooring is one of the most visible and important of all interior design elements.

Flooring can serve as a bold, eye-catching design statement, or it can be an understated background, but whatever approach you take, always consider the design of adjoining rooms when choosing a flooring. Because floors flow from one room to the next, floor coverings offer a convenient medium for creating continuity throughout your home. This does not mean you should use the exact same floor covering everywhere; simply repeating a color, pattern, or texture is often enough.

The examples on these pages help illustrate how your choice of color, pattern, and texture can affect the look and feel of a room.

Floor color influences the visual impact of a room. Bold, bright colors draw attention, while muted colors create a neutral background that does not compete for attention. Colors also affect the perceived size of a room: dark colors are formal in tone, but can make a room look smaller; light colors are more contemporary, and can make the space seem larger.

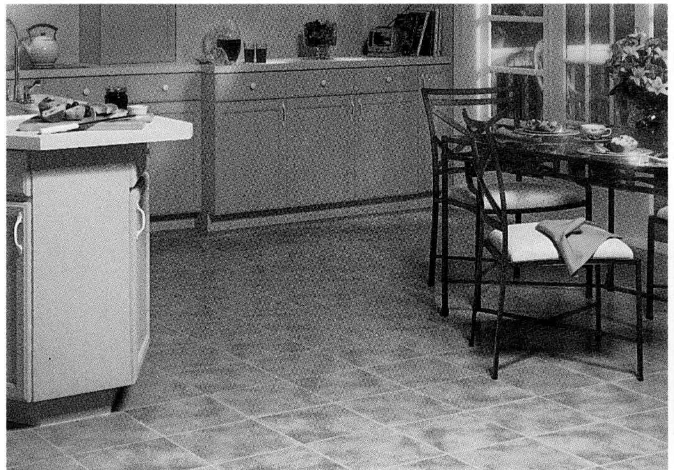

Pattern of flooring materials affects the feeling and tone of a room. In general, subtle patterns lend a more relaxed feel to a room and can make it appear larger. Bold recurring patterns create excitement and focal points for a room. A flooring pattern must be chosen carefully to ensure that it does not clash with other patterns in the room.

Texture of flooring materials contributes to the style of a room. More rugged surfaces, such as slate or berber carpet, give a room a warm, earthy tone. Smooth and glossy surfaces, such as polished marble tile or hardwood flooring, impart an airy sense of elegance.

Determining the number and type of coverings already on your floor is an important first step in evaluating its condition. Too many layers of floor covering and underlayments can stress floor joists and ultimately cause a new floor to fail. An easy way to expose the anatomy of your existing floor is to remove floor vents.

Evaluating an Existing Floor

Taking the time to examine your existing floor is essential before beginning any new floor installation. A careful evaluation will help you make informed decisions on how to prepare the existing floor for the new floor covering.

Evaluating your floor is a three-part process. First, identify the type of existing floor and determine how it was installed: Is your sheet vinyl attached with full-spread adhesive, or is it fastened with perimeter-bond adhesive? Is your carpet glued down, or stretched? Next, assess the condition of the floor: Is it still securely adhered, or is it loose in spots? Is it badly chipped or cracked? Finally, note the height of your existing floor in relation to adjoining floor surfaces.

Quite often, a new floor covering or new underlayment can be installed on top of the existing flooring. Your evaluation, in conjunction with the information in this section, will help you determine if this is possible.

Warning: Resilient flooring manufactured before 1986 contained asbestos, which can cause severe lung problems if inhaled. The recommended method for dealing with asbestos-laden resilient flooring is to cover it with an underlayment. If it must be removed, do not attempt to do the work yourself. Instead, consult a certified asbestos-abatement contractor.

Anatomy of Your Floor

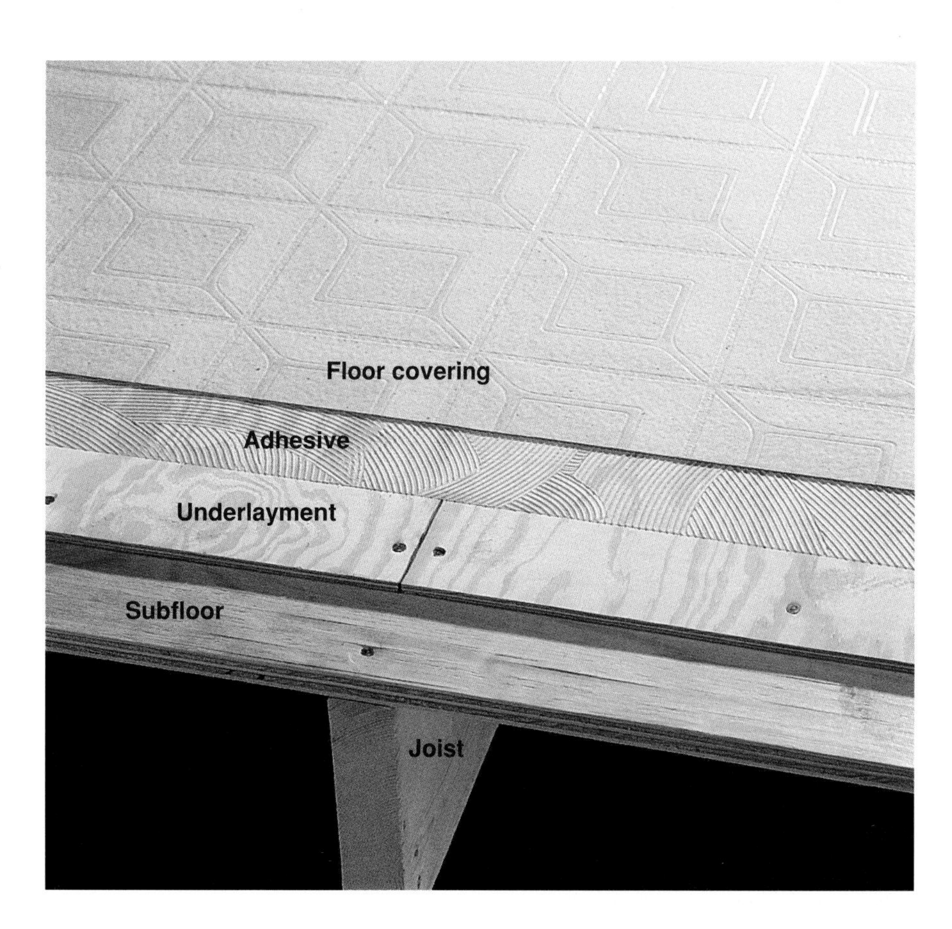

A floor is composed of several layers that work together to provide the required structural support and desired appearance. At the bottom of it all are the joists, the sturdy framing elements that support the weight of the floor. Joists are typically spaced 16" apart on center. Nailed to the joists is the subfloor. Most subfloors installed in the 1970s or later are made of ¾" tongue-and-groove plywood, but in older homes, the subfloor often consists of 1" wood planks nailed diagonally across the floor joists. On top of the subfloor, most builders place a layer of ½" plywood underlayment. For many types of floor coverings, adhesive or mortar is spread on the underlayment before the floor covering is installed.

Tips for Evaluating Floors

Remove enclosed appliances, like dishwashers, if you are planning to lay new flooring over old. Measure the vertical space to make sure the appliances will fit once the new underlayment and flooring are installed. Use samples of the new underlayment and floor covering as spacers when measuring.

Look for high thresholds. They often indicate that several layers of flooring have already been installed on top of one another. If you have several layers, it is best to remove them before installing the new floor covering.

(continued next page)

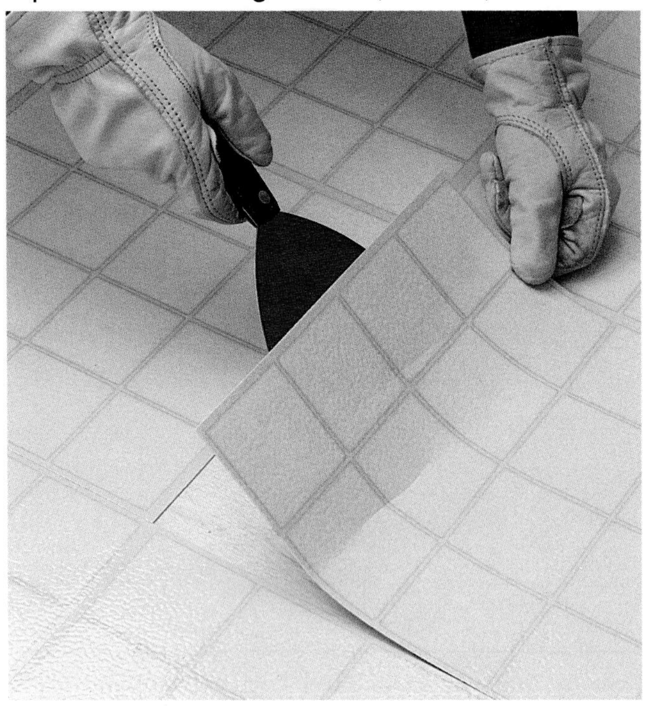

Loose tiles may indicate widespread failure of the adhesive. Use a wallboard knife to test tiles. If tiles can be pried up easily in many different areas of the room, you should plan on removing all the flooring.

Air bubbles trapped under resilient sheet flooring indicate that the adhesive has failed. In this situation, the old flooring must be removed before new flooring can be installed.

Cracks in grout joints around ceramic tile are a sign that movement of the floor covering has caused (or been caused by) deterioration of the adhesive layer. Evaluate the condition of the underlayment (page opposite) to determine if it also must be removed.

Buckling in solid hardwood floors indicates that the boards have loosened from the subfloor. Do not remove hardwood floors; instead, refasten loose areas by drilling pilot holes and driving 8d finish nails into the boards. Before installing resilient floorings or ceramic tile over hardwood, always lay a new underlayment.

A Quick Guide to Evaluating an Existing Floor

Preparing for a new floor can be a simple task or a lengthy, difficult chore, depending on the condition of the existing floor and on your choice of new floor coverings.

The following descriptions summarize the preparation steps for various types of existing floor materials. In some cases, you have several preparation options from which to choose. By carefully considering the options and choosing the most suitable method for your needs, you can avoid wasting time with unnecessary labor. Keep in mind that the goal of any preparation for new flooring is a structurally sound, smooth, and level surface.

FLOORING EVALUATION CHART

Old Resilient Flooring

Option 1: Your existing resilient floor can serve as the foundation for most new floorings, including resilient flooring, hardwood, or carpet, but only if the existing surface is relatively smooth and sound. Inspect the existing flooring for loose seams, tears, chips, air bubbles, and other areas where the bond has failed. If these loose spots constitute less than 30% of the total area, then you can remove the flooring at these spots and fill the voids with floor leveling compound. Apply embossing leveler to the entire surface and let it dry before laying new resilient flooring.

Option 2: If the original resilient flooring is suspect, you can install new underlayment over the old surface after repairing obviously loose areas.

Option 3: If you are installing ceramic tile, or if the existing surface is in very poor condition, the old resilient flooring should be removed entirely before you install new flooring. If the old flooring was glued down with full-bond adhesive, it is usually easiest to remove both the flooring and underlayment at the same time. If the old underlayment is removed, you must install new underlayment before laying the new flooring.

Old Ceramic Tile

Option 1: If the existing ceramic tile surface is relatively solid, new flooring usually can be laid directly over the tile. Inspect tiles and joints for cracks and loose pieces. Remove loose material and fill these areas with a floor leveling compound. If you will be installing resilient flooring, apply an embossing leveler product over the ceramic tile before laying the new flooring. If you will be laying new ceramic tile over the old surface, use an epoxy-based thin-set mortar for better adhesion.

Option 2: If more than 10% of the ceramic tiles are loose, remove all the old flooring before you install the new surface. If the tiles do not easily separate from the underlayment, it is best to remove the ceramic tiles and underlayment at the same time, then install new underlayment.

Old Hardwood Flooring

Option 1: If you are planning to install carpet, you can usually lay it directly over an existing hardwood floor, provided it is a nailed or glued-down surface. Inspect the flooring and secure any loose areas to the subfloor with finish nails, then remove any rotted wood and fill the voids with floor leveling compound before installing carpet.

Option 2: If you will be installing resilient flooring or ceramic tile over nailed hardwood planks or glued-down hardwood flooring, you can attach new underlayment over the existing hardwood before installing the new flooring.

Option 3: If the existing floor is a "floating" hardwood surface with a foam-based underlayment, remove it completely before laying any type of new flooring.

Underlayment & Subfloor

Underlayment must be smooth, solid, and level to ensure a long-lasting flooring installation. If the existing underlayment does not meet these standards, remove it and install new underlayment before you lay new flooring.

Before installing new underlayment, inspect the subfloor for chips, open knots, dips, and loose boards. Screw down loose areas, and fill cracks and dips with floor leveling compound. Remove and replace any water-damaged areas.

Old Carpet

Without exception, carpet must be removed before you install any new flooring. For traditional carpet, simply cut the carpet into pieces, then remove the padding and tackless strips. Remove glued-down cushion-back carpet with a floor scraper, using the same techniques as for removing full-bond resilient sheet flooring (page 32).

Power tools used in floor preparation and installation projects include: power miter saw (A), circular saw (B), power sander (C), jig saw (D), heat gun (E), and cordless drill (F).

Tools for Floor Projects

Many of the hand tools and power tools you will need to successfully complete the flooring projects in this book are probably already in your toolbox or home workshop. Others, such as the power miter box and floor roller are available for lease at rental centers.

For each project, the "Everything You Need" list on the opening page will specify which tools are required. Many of the projects in this book call for basic hand tools. This collection of tools, common to most flooring projects, is listed on the opposite page.

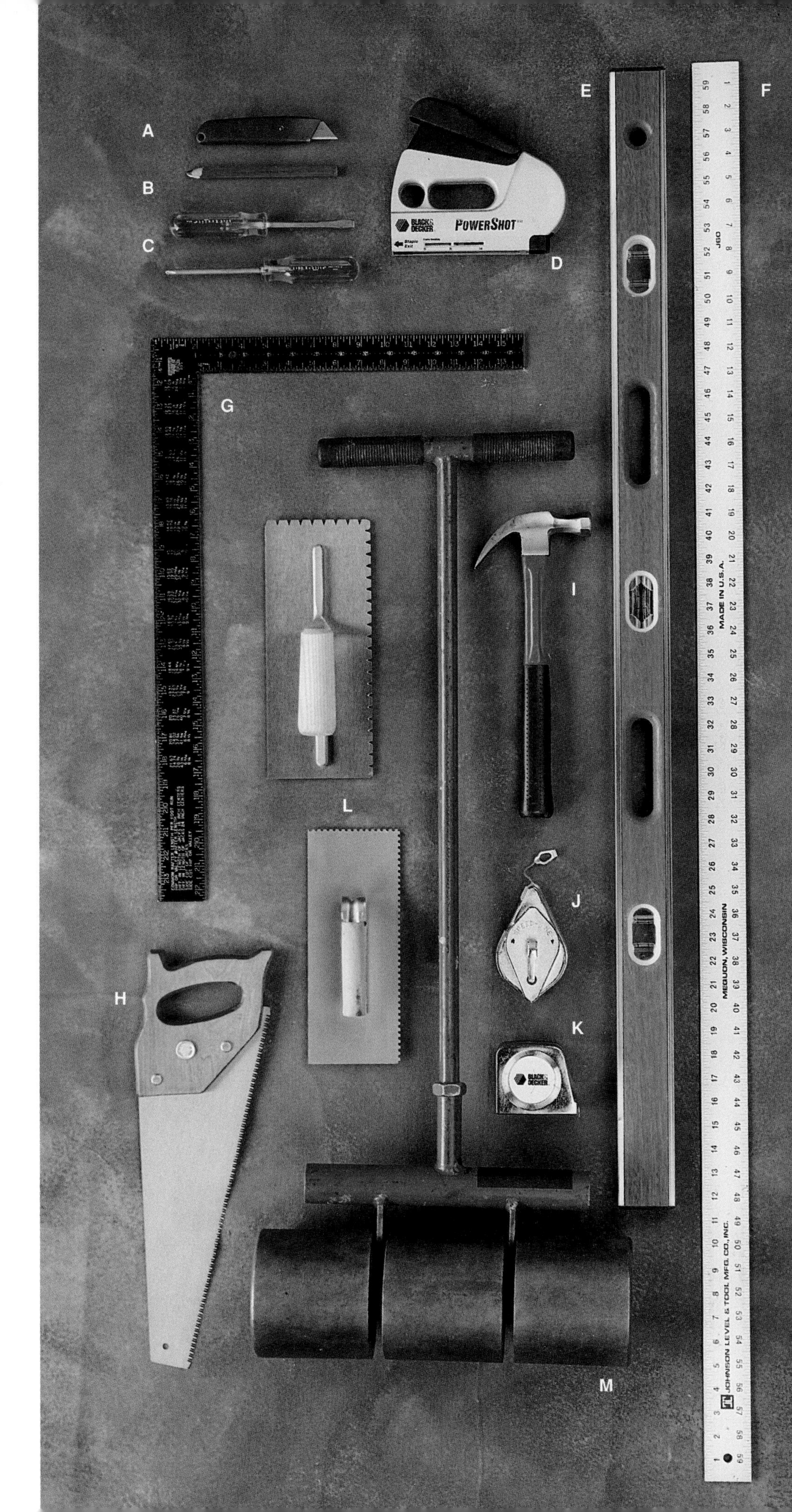

Basic hand tools needed for most floor projects include: utility knife (A), pencil (B), standard and phillips screwdrivers (C), stapler (D), carpenter's level (E), straightedge (F), carpenter's square (G), hand saw (H), hammer (I), chalkline (J), and tape measure (K).

Specialty tools for flooring installation include: notched trowels (L), linoleum roller (M), and others as indicated.

Installing a New Floor: A Step-by-step Overview

Understanding the separate phases of a flooring installation and their relationship to one another will help you manage the job better from start to finish. The sequence shown on these pages will give you a basic overview of a typical installation, though your project may deviate from this sequence.

If your flooring installation is part of a larger remodeling project, see page 25 for guidance on when to schedule the flooring phase.

1 Once you have selected a new flooring to install, evaluate your existing floor to determine whether you can install the new flooring over it (page 25).

2 If necessary, remove the existing flooring to provide a sound surface for your new floor installation (pages 38 to 43).

3 Install the appropriate type of underlayment for your floor covering (pages 44 to 49).

4 Lay out your installation. For resilient or ceramic tile, establish layout lines that divide the room into quadrants (pages 65 to 66). For sheet vinyl, create a template of the room perimeter (page 59). For carpet, determine the positions of seams (page 104).

5 Install your floor covering using the appropriate techniques: resilient flooring (pages 60 to 69), ceramic tile (pages 78 to 85), hardwood flooring (pages 94 to 97), and carpet (pages 115 to 125).

Project Preparation

Project Preparation

Project preparation can range from simple to complex, depending on the condition of your existing floor. As a guide for making preparation decisions, see pages 22 to 25.

Providing a sound, smooth underlayment for your new flooring is a vital preparation step. This may involve only minor modifications to your existing floor, like applying an embossing leveler (page 34). Or, the preparation required may involve complete underlayment removal and spot repairs to your subfloor (pages 42 to 45). Avoid taking shortcuts, because they usually result in an inferior floor. Page 24 shows common results of shortcuts.

If you are installing new underlayment, it is essential that you choose the right material. Page 35 describes the four types of underlayment available.

Before you get started on your floor preparation project, remove appliances or bathroom fixtures and prepare the room for more efficient and comfortable working conditions (pages 36 to 37). Wear safety goggles, work gloves, work boots, and a dust particle mask when doing preparation work.

This sections shows:

Options for Removing Old Flooring

Remove the old floor covering only. If the old underlayment is sturdy and in good condition, you can often get by with simply scraping off the floor covering, then cleaning and reusing the existing underlayment. See pages 38 to 41.

Remove the floor covering and underlayment. If the underlayment is questionable or substandard, remove it along with the old floor covering. Taking up both layers at once saves time. See pages 42 to 43.

Tips for Creating Sturdy Underlayment

Repair and prepare the subfloor. Fix loose boards and other problems before installing your new flooring underlayment. Also use leveling products to fill in dips or gouges. See pages 44 to 45.

Use quality materials. Using a good-quality underlayment appropriate for the flooring you have chosen is critical to the success of your flooring project. See page 35 and pages 46 to 49.

Preparation Tools & Materials

Tools for flooring removal and surface preparation include: a masonry chisel (A), reciprocating saw (B), flat pry bar (C), crowbar (D), long-handled floor scraper (E), utility knife (F), hand maul (G), wallboard knife (H), and cat's paw (I). Specialty tools, such as the floor scraper, are available at rental centers.

How to Use Embossing Leveler

Embossing leveler is a mortarlike substance that can be used to prepare well-adhered resilient flooring or ceramic tile for use as an underlayment for new floor coverings. Mix leveler according to manufacturer's directions and spread thinly over the floor with a flat-edged trowel. Wipe away any excess with the trowel, making sure all dips and indentations remain filled. Work quickly—embossing leveler begins setting up in 10 minutes. After the leveler dries, scrape away ridges and high spots with the trowel edge.

Selecting Underlayment Materials

Which type of underlayment you should choose depends in part on the type of floor covering you will be installing. For example, ceramic and natural-stone floors require a rigid and stable underlayment that resists movement, such as cementboard. For resilient flooring, use a quality-grade plywood, since most manufacturers will void their warranty if their flooring is installed over substandard underlayment. Solid wood strip flooring and carpet do not require underlayment and are often placed directly on a plywood subfloor.

Plywood (A) is the most common underlayment for resilient flooring and ceramic tile installations. For resilient flooring, use ¼" exterior-grade, AC plywood (at least one side perfectly smooth). Wood-based floor coverings, like parquet, can be installed over lower-quality exterior-grade plywood. For ceramic tile, use ½" AC plywood. Most manufacturers now recommend plywood over other wood-based, sheet-good underlayments.

Fiber/cementboard (B) is a thin, high-density underlayment used under ceramic tile and resilient flooring in situations where floor height is a concern. (For installation, follow steps for cementboard installation, page 48.)

Cementboard (C) is used only for ceramic tile installations. It is completely stable, even when wet, and is therefore the best underlayment to use in areas likely to get wet, such as bathrooms. Cementboard is considerably more expensive than plywood.

Isolation membrane (D) is used to protect ceramic tile installations from movement that may occur on cracked concrete floors. It is used primarily for covering individual cracks with strips of membrane, but it can also be used over an entire floor. A specialty product, it is available from commercial tile distributors.

Latex patching compounds can be used to fill cracks and chips in old underlayment as well as to cover screw or nail heads and seams in new underlayment. Some products include separate dry and wet ingredients that need to be mixed before application; others are premixed.

Tips for Getting Ready for a Flooring Project

Disconnect and remove all appliances. When putting appliances back in place, protect your new floor by laying cardboard or heavy cloth in front of the appliance location. Before repositioning appliances, make sure the floor adhesives are properly cured.

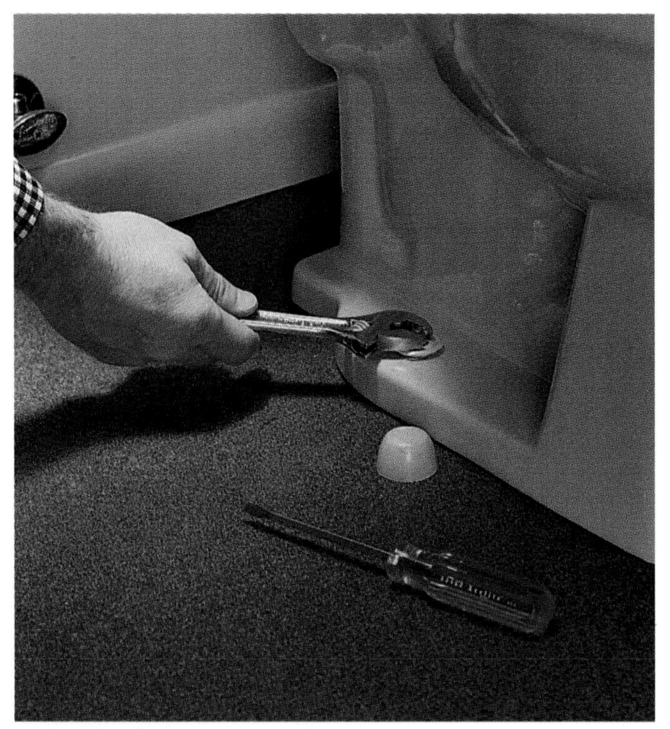

Remove the toilet and any other floor-mounted fixtures before installing bathroom flooring. Turn off and disconnect the water supply line, then remove the bolts holding the toilet to floor (see Black & Decker® Home Improvement Library's *Bathroom Remodeling*).

Remove base moldings before preparing for ceramic, resilient, and hardwood flooring installation. Carefully pry the moldings from the wall with a flat pry bar, using a wallboard knife to protect wall surfaces. Number each piece to simplify reinstallation.

Undercut door casings with a hand saw to make room for thicker floor products. For vinyl and wood, use a scrap of underlayment and a piece of new flooring as a spacing guide. For ceramic tile, also take into account the height of the adhesive.

Ventilate the project room, especially when applying adhesives or removing old flooring. A box fan placed in an open window and directed outside creates good air movement.

Shovel old flooring debris from your house through a window and into a wheelbarrow to speed up removal work. Protect fragile plants near the window with sheets of plywood.

Cover doorways with sheet plastic to contain debris and dust during removal.

Cover air and heat vents with sheet plastic and masking tape to prevent dust from entering ductwork.

Use a floor scraper to remove resilient flooring products, and to scrape off leftover adhesives or backings. The long handle provides leverage and force, and allows you to work in a comfortable standing position. A scraper will remove most flooring, but you may need to use other tools to finish the job.

Removing Floor Coverings

When old floor coverings must be removed—as is the case with most projects—thorough and careful removal work is essential to the quality of the new flooring installation.

The difficulty of flooring removal depends on the type of floor covering and the method that was used to install it. Carpet and perimeter-bond vinyl are generally quite easy to remove, and vinyl tiles are relatively simple. Full-spread sheet vinyl can be difficult to remove, however, and ceramic tile removal is always challenging.

With any removal, be sure to keep tool blades sharp and try to avoid damaging the underlayment.

Everything You Need:

Tools: basic hand tools (page 27); floor scraper, eye protection, wallboard knife, spray bottle, heat gun (for resilient flooring removal); hand maul, masonry chisel (for ceramic tile removal); pry bar, end-cutting nippers (for carpet removal).

How to Remove Sheet Vinyl

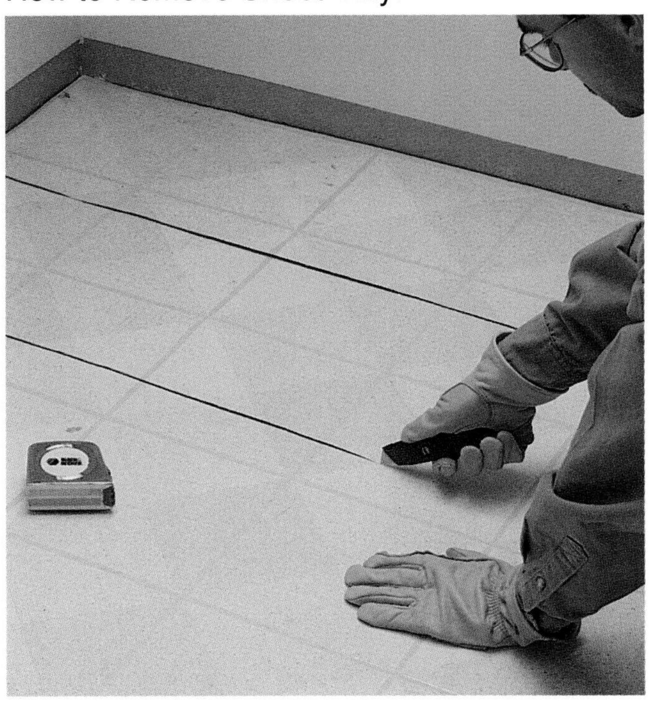

1 Use a utility knife to cut old flooring into strips about a foot wide. This makes removal considerably easier.

2 Pull up as much flooring as possible by hand.

3 Cut stubborn sheet vinyl into strips about 5" wide. Starting at a wall, peel up as much of the floor covering as possible. If felt backing remains, spray a solution of water and liquid dishwashing detergent under the surface layer to help separate felt backing. Use a wallboard knife to scrape up particularly stubborn patches.

4 Scrape up remaining sheet vinyl and backing, using a floor scraper. If necessary, spray the backing again with soap solution to loosen it. Sweep up debris, then finish the cleanup with a wet/dry vacuum. TIP: Fill shop vac with about an inch of water to keep dust at bay.

How to Remove Vinyl Tiles

1 Starting at a loose seam, use a long-handled floor scraper to remove tiles. To remove stubborn tiles, soften the adhesive with a heat gun, then use a wallboard knife to pry up the tile and scrape off the underlying adhesive.

2 Remove stubborn adhesive or backing by wetting the floor with a water/detergent mixture, then scraping with a floor scraper.

How to Remove Ceramic Tile

1 Knock out tile using a hand maul and masonry chisel. If possible, start in a space between tiles where grout has loosened. Be careful when working around fragile fixtures, like drain flanges.

2 If you plan to reuse the underlayment, use a floor scraper to remove any remaining adhesive. You may have to use a belt sander with a coarse sanding belt to grind off stubborn adhesive.

How to Remove Carpet

1 Using a utility knife, cut around metal threshold strips to free carpet. Remove threshold strips with a flat pry bar.

2 Cut carpet into pieces small enough to be easily removed. Roll up carpet and remove it from the room, then remove the padding. NOTE: Padding is usually stapled to the floor, and will typically come up in pieces as you roll it up.

3 Using end-cutting nippers or pliers, remove all staples from floor. TIP: If you plan to lay new carpet, do not remove tackless strips unless they are damaged.

OPTION: To remove glued-down carpet, first cut it into strips with a utility knife, then pull up as much material as you can. Scrape up remaining cushion material and adhesive with a floor scraper.

Remove underlayment and floor covering as if they were a single layer. This is an effective removal strategy with any floor covering that is bonded to the underlayment.

Removing Underlayment

Flooring contractors routinely remove the underlayment along with the floor covering before installing new flooring. This saves time and makes it possible to install new underlayment ideally suited to the new flooring. Do-it-yourselfers using this technique should make sure they cut flooring into manageable pieces that can be easily handled.

Warning: This floor removal method releases flooring particles into the air. Be sure the vinyl you are removing does not contain asbestos (page 22).

Everything You Need:

Tools: eye protection, circular saw, reciprocating saw, wood chisel, hand maul, masonry chisel, pry bar.

Removal Tip

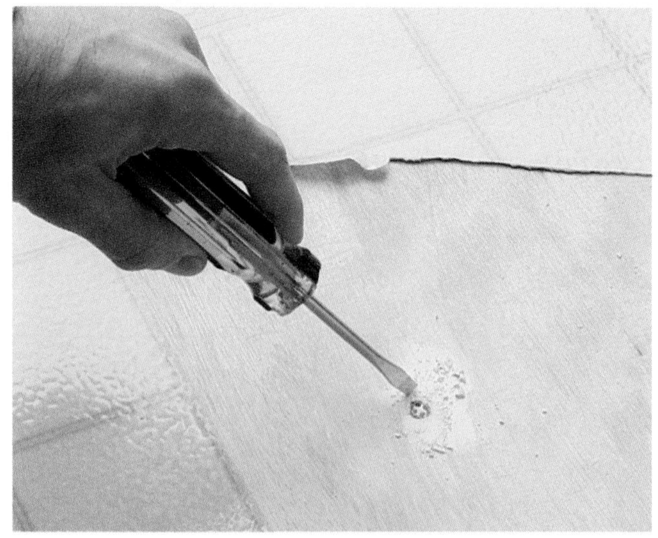

Examine fasteners to see how the underlayment is attached. Use a screwdriver to expose the heads of the fasteners. If the underlayment has been screwed down, you will need to remove the floor covering before you can unscrew the underlayment.

How to Remove Underlayment

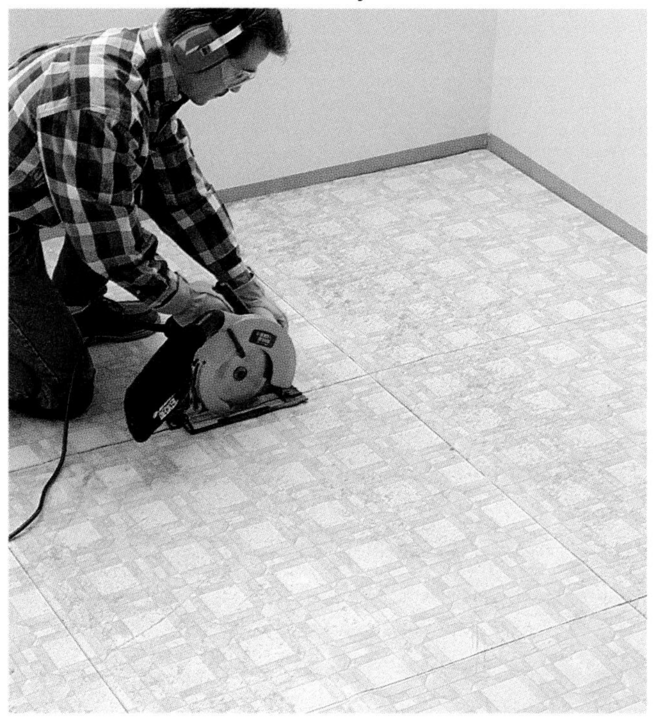

1 Adjust the cutting depth of a circular saw to equal the combined thickness of your floor covering and underlayment. Using a carbide-tipped blade, cut the floor covering and underlayment into squares measuring about 3 ft. square. Be sure to wear safety goggles and gloves.

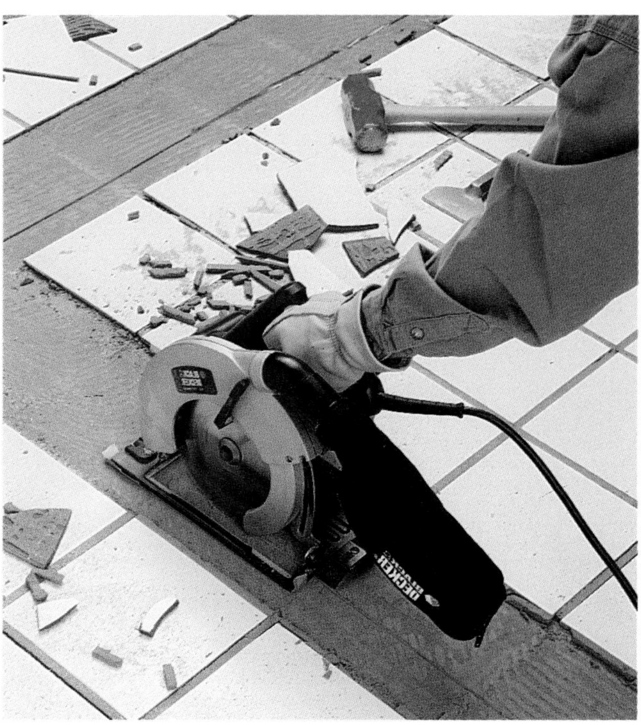

VARIATION: If your existing floor is ceramic tile over plywood underlayment, use a hand maul and masonry chisel to chip away tile along cutting lines before making cuts.

2 Use a reciprocating saw to extend cuts close to the edges of walls. Hold the blade at a slight angle to the floor, and try not to damage walls or cabinets. Use a wood chisel to complete cuts near cabinets.

3 Separate underlayment from subfloor, using a flat pry bar and hammer. Remove and discard the sections of underlayment and floor covering immediately, watching for exposed nails.

Refasten loose subfloor material. Before installing new underlayment and floor covering, refasten any sections of loose subfloor to floor joists using deck screws.

Repairing Subfloors

A solid, securely fastened subfloor minimizes floor movement and ensures that your new floor will last a long time. After removing old underlayment, inspect the subfloor for loose seams, moisture damage, cracks, and other flaws. If your subfloor is made of dimensional lumber rather than plywood, you can use plywood to patch damaged sections; if the plywood patch does not quite match the height of the subfloor, use floor leveler to raise its surface to the correct height.

Everything You Need:

Tools: basic hand tools (page 27), flat trowel, drill with phillips head, circular saw, cat's paw.

Materials: floor leveler, 2" deck screws, plywood, 2 x 4 lumber.

Repair Tip

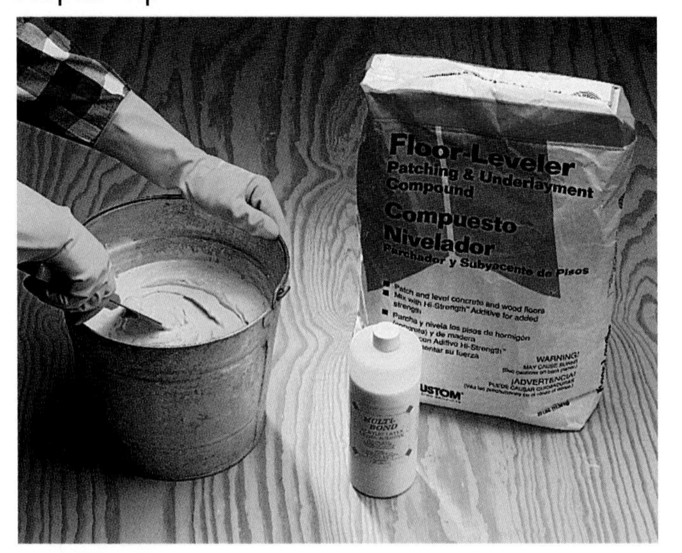

Floor leveler is used to fill in dips and low spots in plywood subfloors. Using a latex or acrylic additive, mix the leveler according to the manufacturer's directions.

How to Apply Floor Leveler

1 Fill dips, chips, or cracks in the subfloor with floor leveler. Mix leveler according to manufacturer's directions, then spread it on the subfloor with a trowel.

2 Check with a straightedge to make sure the filled area is even with the surrounding area; if not, apply more leveler. Allow leveler to dry, then shave off any ridges with the edge of a trowel, or sand smooth, if necessary.

How to Replace a Section of Subfloor

1 Mark, cut, and remove damaged areas. Mark a rectangle around the damage, with two sides centered over floor joists. Cut, using a circular saw with the blade adjusted to cut only through the subfloor. Use a chisel to complete cuts near walls.

2 Remove damaged section, then nail two 2 × 4 blocks between joists, centered under the cut edges for added support. If possible, end-nail blocks from below; otherwise toe-nail them from above.

3 Measure the cut-out section, then cut to fit, using material the same thickness as the original subfloor. Fasten to joists and blocks, using 2" deck screws spaced about 5" apart.

Install new plywood underlayment to provide the best possible base for gluing down resilient flooring or ceramic tile. Cut the plywood to fit around moldings and other room contours.

Installing Underlayment

When installing underlayment, make sure it is securely attached to the subfloor in all areas, including below all movable appliances. Notching the underlayment to properly fit room contours is often the most challenging step. Take time to measure carefully and transfer the correct measurements onto your underlayment. Rather than notching around door casings, you can undercut the casings and insert the underlayment beneath them (page 36).

For help in selecting the appropriate underlayment for your new flooring, see the guide on page 35.

Everything You Need:

Tools: basic hand tools (page 27); drill with phillips bit, circular saw, wallboard knife, power sander (for plywood); countersink drill bit (for high-density fiberboard); jig saw with carbide blade (for cementboard); ¼" notched trowel (for cementboard); ⅛" notched trowel, linoleum roller (for isolation membrane).

Materials: underlayment; 1" deck screws, latex patching compound (for plywood and high-density); dry-set mortar (for cementboard and isolation membrane).

How to Install Plywood Underlayment

1 Begin installing full sheets of plywood along the longest wall, making sure underlayment seams are not aligned with subfloor seams. Fasten plywood to the subfloor, using 1" screws driven every 6" along the edges and at 8" intervals throughout the rest of the sheet.

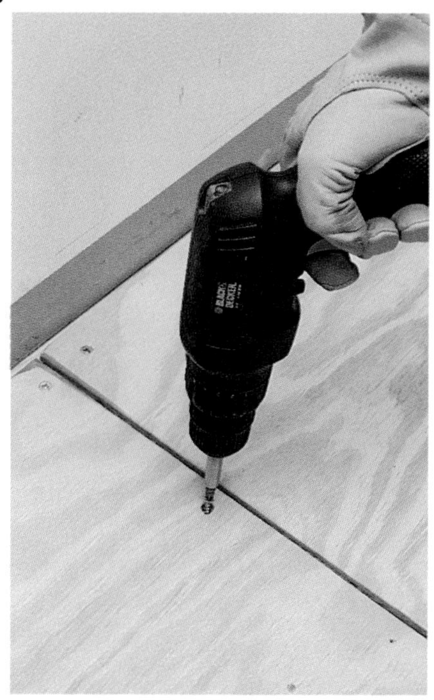

2 Continue fastening plywood to the subfloor, driving screw heads slightly below the underlayment surface. Leave ¼" expansion gaps at the walls and between sheets. Offset seams in subsequent rows.

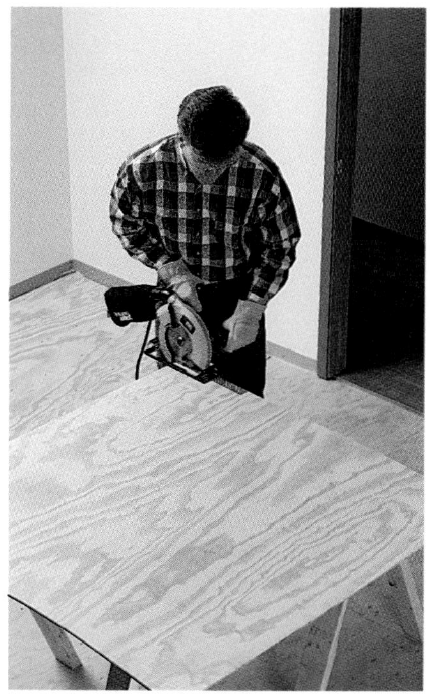

3 Using a circular saw or jig saw, notch underlayment sheets to meet existing flooring in doorways, then fasten notched sheets to the subfloor.

4 Mix floor patching compound and latex or acrylic additive, according to manufacturer's directions. Then, spread it over seams and screw heads with a wallboard knife.

5 Let patching compound dry, then sand patched areas smooth, using a power sander.

How to Install Cementboard or Fiber/Cementboard Underlayment

1 Mix thin-set mortar according to manufacturer's recommendations. Starting at the longest wall, spread mortar on subfloor in a figure-eight pattern with a ¼" notched trowel. Spread only enough mortar for one sheet at a time. Set the cementboard sheet on the mortar, smooth-face up, making sure the edges are offset from subfloor seams.

2 Fasten cementboard to subfloor, using 1½" deck screws driven every 6" along edges and 8" throughout sheet; drive screw heads flush with surface. Continue spreading mortar and installing sheets along the wall. OPTION: If installing fiber/cement underlayment, use a 3⁄16" notched trowel to spread mortar, and drill pilot holes for all screws.

3 Cut cementboard pieces to fit, leaving a slight gap at the joints. For straight cuts, score a line with a utility knife, then snap the board along the score.

4 To cut holes, notches, or irregular shapes, use a jig saw with a carbide blade. Continue installing cementboard sheets to cover the entire floor.

5 Place fiberglass mesh tape over seams, and spread a thin layer of thin-set mortar over the tape with a wallboard knife, feathering the edges. Allow mortar to cure for two days before proceeding with tile installation.

How to Install Isolation Membrane

1 Thoroughly clean the subfloor, then apply thin-set mortar with a ⅛" notched trowel. Start spreading the mortar along a wall in a section as wide as the membrane, and 8 to 10 ft. long. NOTE: For some membranes, you must use a bonding material other than mortar. Read the directions on the label.

2 Roll out the membrane over the mortar. Cut the membrane to fit tightly against the walls, using a straightedge and utility knife.

3 Starting in the center of the membrane, use a linoleum roller to smooth out the surface toward the edges. This frees trapped air and presses out excess bonding material.

4 Repeat steps 1 through 3, cutting membrane as necessary at the walls, until the floor is completely covered with membrane. Do not overlap seams, but make sure they are tight. Allow mortar to cure for two days before installing tile.

Installing Floor Coverings

Floor covering projects can be as straightforward as laying down self-adhesive vinyl tile or as elaborate as using ceramic tile to create a diamond-shaped design inside a tile border, as shown above.

Installing Floor Coverings

This section describes the tools, techniques, and materials needed to install resilient vinyl flooring, ceramic tile, and hardwood flooring. For each flooring type, you have several options when choosing materials and installation methods. For a description of these options, see the facing page and refer to the individual section covering each flooring type.

This section shows:

Options for Installing Floor Coverings

Resilient sheet vinyl can be installed fairly easily, using the perimeter-bond method (pages 60 to 62). Full-spread installations (page 63) are more time-consuming.

Resilient tile with self-adhesive backing is probably the easiest of all floor coverings to install (pages 67 to 69). Dry-back resilient tiles are also easy to install, though slightly more time-consuming, since they require spreading adhesive on the floor (page 69).

Ceramic tile normally is square and installed in a simple grid pattern (pages 78 to 85). However, special techniques and non-square tile shapes can be used to create more elaborate designs (pages 86 to 89).

Manufactured hardwood flooring installation methods are easier and faster than the traditional nail-down method used for solid hardwood flooring. Manufactured flooring material can either be glued directly to the floor (pages 94 to 96) or "floated" on a pad (page 97).

Most resilient flooring is made at least in part from vinyl. In general, the higher the percentage of vinyl in the product, the higher the quality of the tile. In solid vinyl flooring, the design pattern is built up from solid layers of vinyl. Vinyl composition flooring combines vinyl with filler materials. Printed vinyl flooring relies on a screen print for its color and pattern; the print is protected by a vinyl and urethane wear layer.

Resilient Flooring

Resilient flooring is often designed to mimic the look of ceramic tile or terrazzo, but is much easier to install and far less expensive. It is available both in sheets and tiles. Sheet vinyl comes in 6- and 12-foot-wide rolls. Most vinyl tiles are 1-foot squares, though some manufacturers make 9-inch square tiles and thin, 2-foot-long border strips.

Sheet vinyl is a good choice for bathrooms, kitchens, and other moist locations, since it has few seams for water to seep through; in smaller rooms, you can install sheet vinyl with no seams at all. Vinyl tiles perform best in dry locations, where a floor with many seams is not a liability.

The quality of resilient flooring varies significantly, and is based primarily on the amount of vinyl in the material. Solid vinyl is the best and most expensive flooring. In this type, the pattern is created by embedding colored vinyl pieces in a vinyl base. Vinyl composition products are less expensive than solid vinyl products. In composition flooring, the pattern is created by fusing colored vinyl with nonvinyl fillers. With both solid vinyl and vinyl composition flooring, the thickness of the flooring is a good clue to its quality; thicker materials have more vinyl and are therefore more durable.

Unlike traditional solid and composition vinyl materials, printed flooring gets its color and pattern from the print itself, which has no vinyl content. Instead, printed flooring is manufactured with a wear layer of urethane and vinyl. The thicker the wear layer, the better the quality of the flooring. When shopping, inspect and compare materials, and ask the sales representative for information.

Resilient sheet vinyl comes in full-spread and perimeter-bond styles. Full-spread sheet vinyl has a felt-paper backing, and is secured with adhesive that is spread over the floor before installation. Perimeter-bond flooring, identifiable by its smooth, white PVC backing, is laid directly on underlayment and is secured by a special adhesive spread along the edges and seams.

Full-spread vinyl flooring bonds tightly to the floor and is unlikely to come loose, but it is more difficult to install and requires a flawlessly smooth and clean underlayment.

Perimeter-bond flooring, by contrast, is easier to install and will tolerate some minor underlayment flaws. However, it is also more likely to come loose.

Resilient tile comes in self-adhesive and dry-back styles. Self-adhesive tile has a preapplied adhesive protected by a wax-paper backing that is peeled off as the tiles are installed. Dry-back tile is secured with adhesive spread onto the underlayment before installation.

Self-adhesive tile is easier to install than dry-back tile, but the bond is less reliable. Do not use additional adhesives with self-adhesive tile.

Tips for Working with Resilient Flooring

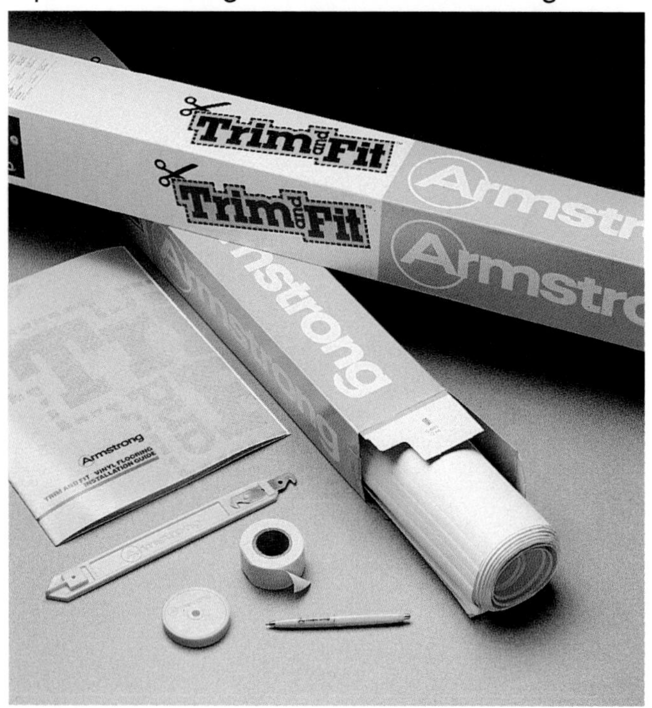

Make a template of the room perimeter to ensure an exact fit for a sheet vinyl installation. Some flooring manufacturers offer template kits and may even guarantee the installation if you use their kit.

Use a linoleum knife or a utility knife to cut resilient flooring. Make sure the knife blade is sharp, and change blades often. Always make cuts on a smooth surface, such as a scrap of hardboard.

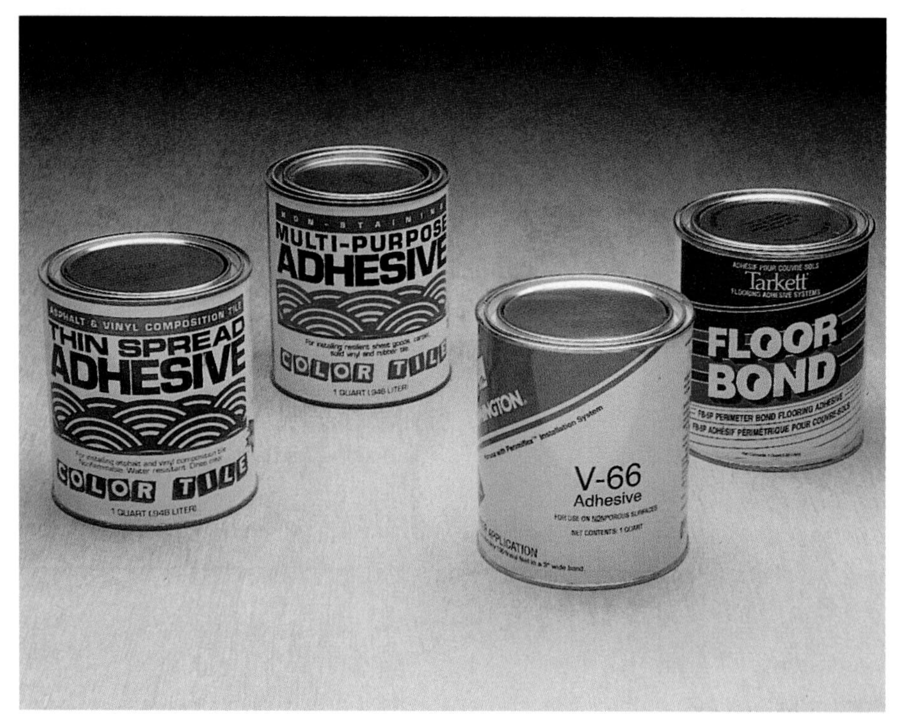

Use the appropriate adhesive for the type of resilient flooring you are installing. Use thin-spread adhesive for installing vinyl composition flooring and multipurpose adhesive for solid vinyl tiles and full-spread sheet vinyl. Manufacturers of perimeter-bond sheet vinyl usually require you to use their proprietary adhesives to qualify for product warranties. They sell two kinds: one for installations on underlayment and another for installations on nonporous surfaces, such as sheet vinyl.

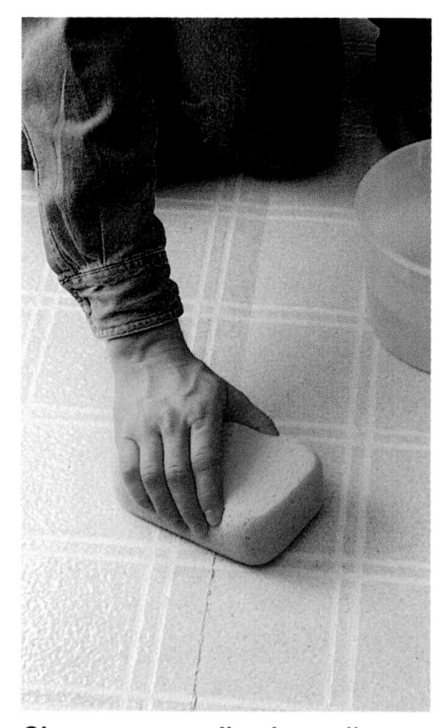

Clean excess adhesives off your new flooring immediately. Use soapy warm water for water-based adhesive. Isopropyl alcohol will remove most perimeter glues, as well as dried-on water-based adhesives.

Sweep and vacuum underlayment thoroughly before installing resilient flooring to ensure a smooth, flawless finish (left). Small pieces of debris can create noticeable bumps in the flooring (right).

Handle resilient sheet vinyl carefully to avoid creasing or tearing it (inset). Working with a helper can help prevent costly mistakes. Make sure the sheet vinyl is at room temperature before you handle it.

Installing Resilient Sheet Vinyl

The most important phase of a sheet vinyl installation is creating a near-perfect underlayment surface. Another key to a successful installation is cutting the material so it fits perfectly along the contours of a room. Making a cutting template is the best way to ensure that your cuts will be correct (opposite page). When handling sheet vinyl, remember that this product—especially felt-backed—can crease and tear easily if mishandled.

Make sure you use the recommended adhesive for the sheet vinyl you are installing. Many manufacturers require that you use their glue to install their flooring, and will void their warranties if you do not follow their directions exactly. Apply adhesive sparingly, using a ⅛ or ¼" trowel.

Everything You Need:

Tools: basic hand tools (page 27), linoleum knife, compass, scissors, wallboard knife, J-roller, 100-lb. floor roller (for full-spread).

Materials: template paper, masking tape, duct tape, flooring adhesive, metal threshold.

How to Make a Cutting Template

1 Place sheets of heavy butcher's or postal-wrap paper along the walls, leaving a ⅛" gap. Cut triangular holes in the paper with a utility knife. Fasten the template to the floor by placing masking tape over the holes.

2 Follow the outline of the room, working with one sheet of paper at a time. Overlap the edges of adjoining sheets by about 2", and tape the sheets together.

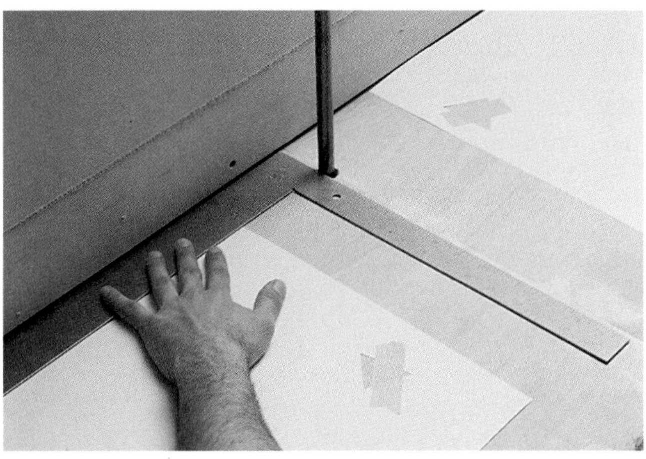

3 To fit the template around pipes, tape sheets of paper on either side. Measure the distance from the wall to the center of the pipe, and subtract ⅛".

4 Transfer the measurement to a separate piece of paper. Use a compass to draw the pipe diameter onto the paper, then cut out the hole with scissors or a utility knife. Cut a slit from the edge of the paper to the hole.

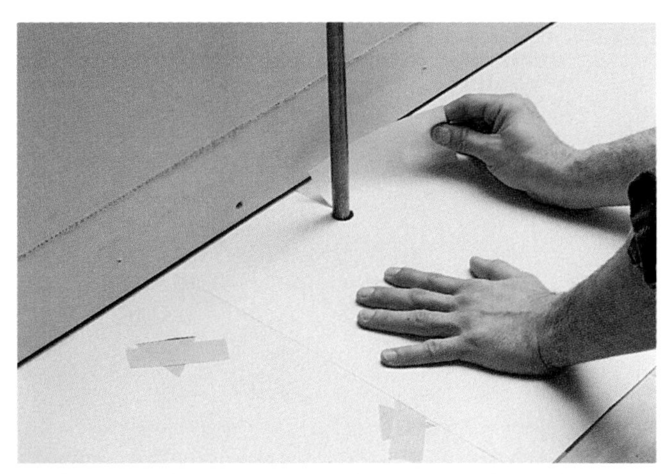

5 Fit the hole cutout around the pipe. Tape the hole template to adjoining sheets.

6 When completed, roll or loosely fold the paper template for carrying.

How to Install Perimeter-bond Sheet Vinyl

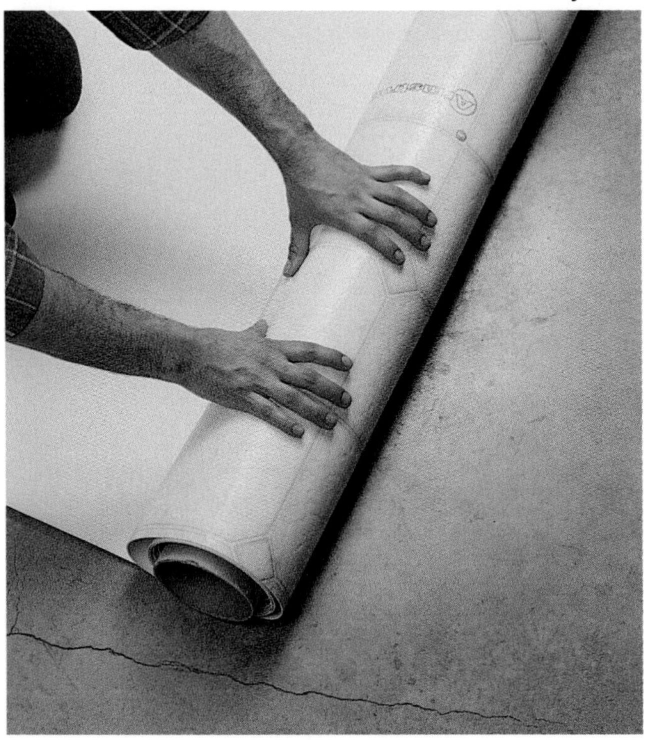

1 Unroll the flooring on any large, flat, clean surface. To prevent wrinkles, sheet vinyl comes from the manufacturer rolled with the pattern side out. Unroll the sheet and turn it pattern-side up for marking.

2 For two-piece installations, overlap the edges of sheets by at least 2". Plan seams to fall along the pattern lines or simulated grout joints. Align the sheets so that the pattern matches, then tape the sheets together with duct tape.

3 Position the paper template over the sheet vinyl, and tape it into place. Trace the outline of the template onto the flooring with a nonpermanent, felt-tipped pen.

4 Remove the template. Cut the sheet vinyl with a sharp linoleum knife, or a utility knife with a new sharp blade. Use a straightedge as a guide for making longer cuts.

5 Cut holes for pipes and other permanent obstructions. Then cut a slit from the hole to the nearest edge of the flooring. Make slits along pattern lines, if possible.

6 Roll up flooring loosely and transfer it to the installation area. Do not fold flooring. Unroll and position the sheet vinyl carefully. Slide the edges beneath undercut door casings (page 36).

7 Cut seams for two-piece installations, using a straightedge as a guide. Hold the straightedge tightly against the flooring, and cut along the pattern lines through both pieces of vinyl flooring.

8 Remove both pieces of scrap flooring. The pattern should now run continuously across the adjoining sheets of flooring.

(continued next page)

How to Install Perimeter-bond Sheet Vinyl (continued)

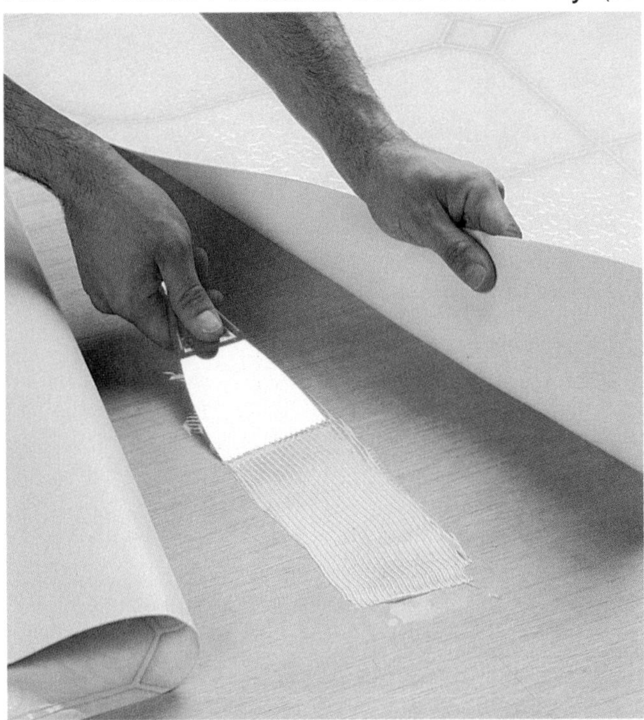

9 Fold back the edges of both sheets and apply a 3" band of multipurpose flooring adhesive (page 56) to the underlayment or old flooring, using a wallboard knife or ¼" notched trowel.

10 Lay seam edges one at a time into the adhesive. Make sure the seam is tight, pressing gaps together with your fingers, if needed. Roll the seam edges with a J-roller or wallpaper seam roller.

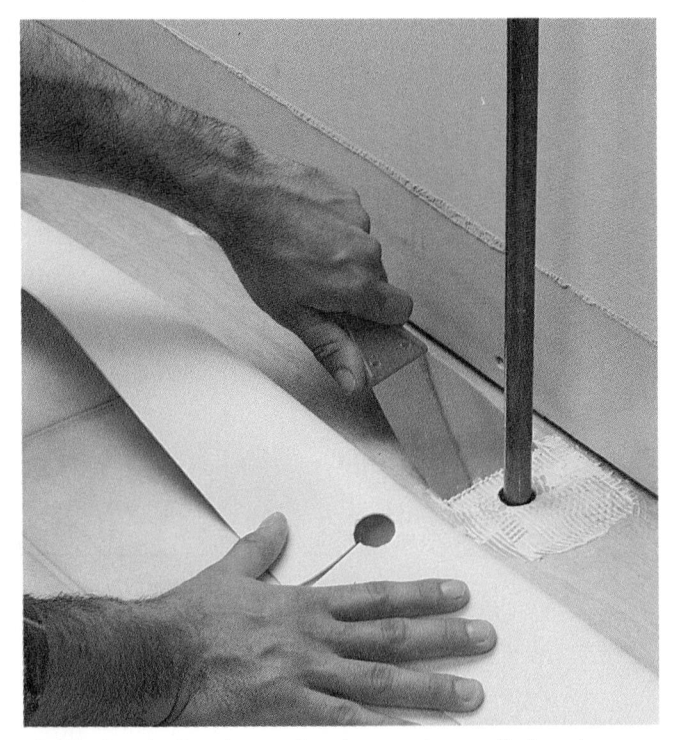

11 Apply flooring adhesive underneath flooring cuts at pipes or posts and around the entire perimeter of the room. Roll the flooring with the roller to ensure good contact with the adhesive.

12 If applying flooring over a wood underlayment, fasten the outer edges of the sheet to the floor with ⅜" staples driven every 3". Make sure the staples will be covered by the wall base molding.

How to Install Full-spread Sheet Vinyl

1 Cut the sheet vinyl using the techniques described on pages 60 and 61 (steps 1 to 5), then lay the sheet vinyl into position, sliding the edges underneath door casings.

2 Pull back half of the flooring, then apply a layer of flooring adhesive over the underlayment or old flooring, using a ¼" notched trowel. Lay the flooring back onto the adhesive.

3 Roll the floor with a floor roller, moving toward the edges of the sheet. The roller creates a stronger bond and eliminates air bubbles. Fold over the unbonded section of flooring, apply adhesive, then lay and roll the flooring. Wipe up any adhesive that oozes up around the edges of the vinyl, using a damp rag.

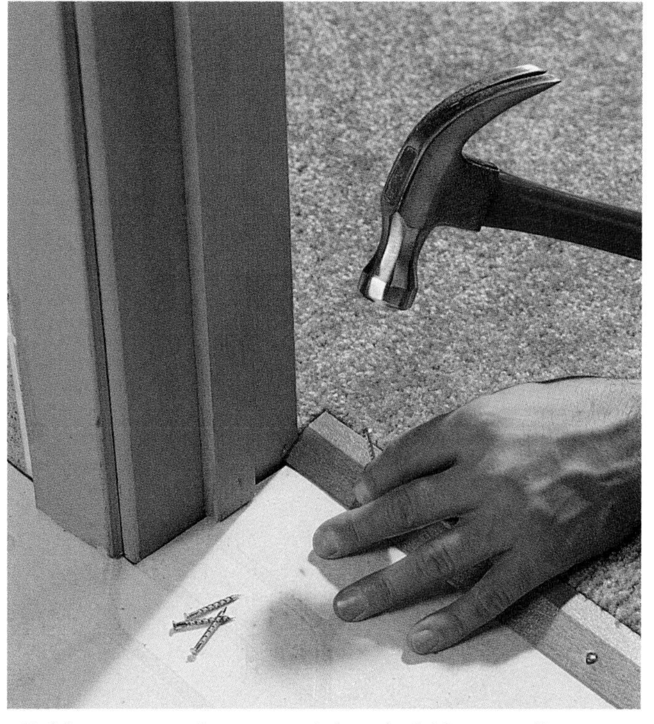

4 Measure and cut metal threshold bars to fit across doorways, then position each bar over the edge of the vinyl flooring and nail it in place.

Installing Resilient Tile

When installing self-adhesive resilient tile, install all full tiles in each layout quadrant first, then cut and install all partial tiles.

The key to a great-looking resilient tile installation is carefully positioning the layout lines. Once the layout lines are established, the actual installation of the tile is relatively easy, especially if you are using self-adhesive tile. Before committing to any layout, however, be sure to dry-fit the tiles to identify potential problems.

Tiles with an obvious grain pattern can be laid so the grain of each tile is oriented identically throughout the installation. Or, you can use the quarter-turn method, in which each tile is laid with its pattern grain running perpendicular to that of adjacent tiles.

Everything You Need:

Tools: basic hand tools (page 27), 1⁄16" notched trowel (for dry-back tile).

Materials: resilient tile, flooring adhesive (for dry-back tile).

Tips for Installing Resilient Tile

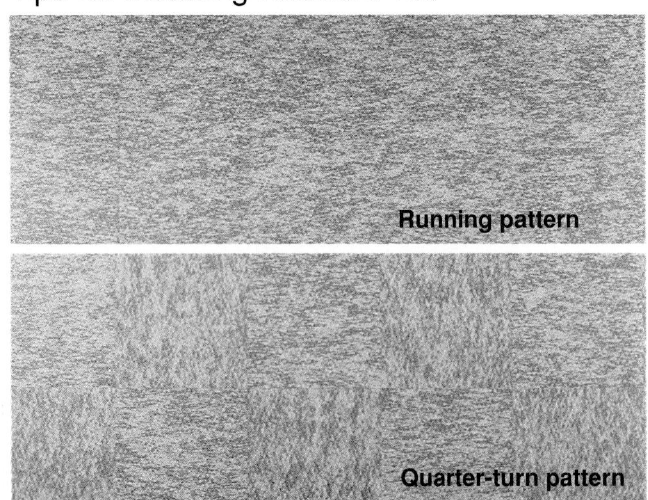

Check for noticeable directional features, like the grain of the vinyl particles. You can choose to set the tile in a running pattern, so the directional feature runs in the same direction (top), or you can set the tiles in a checkerboard pattern, called the quarter-turn method (bottom).

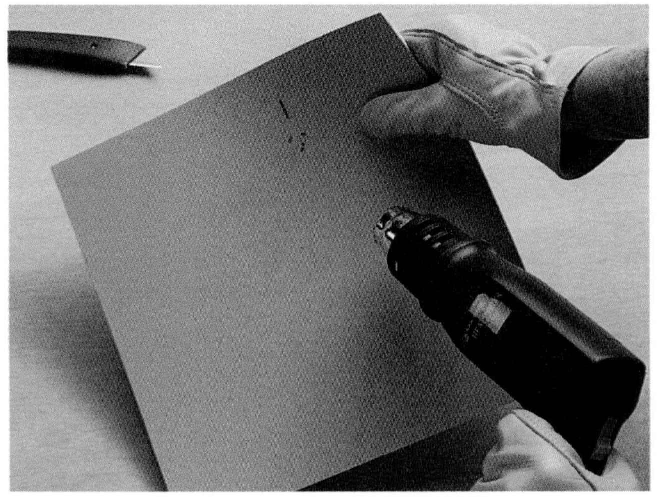

Make curved cuts in thick, rigid resilient tile by heating the back of the tile with a heat gun first, then cutting it while it is still warm.

How to Establish Perpendicular Reference Lines for a Tile Installation

1 Position a reference line (X) by measuring opposite sides of the room and marking the center of each side. Snap a chalk line between these marks.

2 Measure and mark the centerpoint of the chalk line. From this point, use a framing square to establish a second line perpendicular to the first. Snap a second reference line (Y) across the room.

3 Check for squareness using the "3-4-5 triangle" method. Measure and mark one reference line 3 ft. from the centerpoint on line X. Measure and mark the other reference line 4 ft. from the centerpoint on line Y. Measure the distance between the marks. If reference lines are perpendicular, the distance will measure exactly 5 ft. If not, adjust the reference lines until they are exactly perpendicular to one another.

How to Establish Tile Layout Lines

1 Snap perpendicular reference lines (X, Y) with a chalk line (see previous page). Dry-fit tiles along one perpendicular layout line (Y). If necessary, you can shift the layout one way or the other to make the layout visually symmetrical or to reduce the number of tiles that need to be cut.

2 If you have shifted the tile layout, create a new line that is parallel to reference line X and runs through a tile joint near the original line. This new line (X′) will be one of the layout lines you will use when installing the tile. NOTE: To avoid confusion, use a different-colored chalk to distinguish between the original reference line and the new layout line.

3 Dry-fit tiles along the new layout line (X′). If necessary, adjust the layout, as in steps 1 and 2.

4 If you have adjusted the layout along line X′, measure and mark a new layout line (Y′) that is parallel to the reference line (Y) and runs through one of the tile joints. This new line will form the second layout line you will use during the installation.

How to Install Self-adhesive Resilient Tiles

1 Draw reference and layout lines (previous page), then peel off the paper backing and install the first tile in one of the corners formed by the intersecting layout lines. Lay three or more tiles along each layout line in the quadrant. Rub the entire surface of each tile to bond the adhesive to the floor underlayment.

2 Begin installing tiles in the interior area of the quadrant, making sure to keep the joints between tiles tight.

3 Finish setting full-size tiles in the first quadrant, then set the full-size tiles in an adjacent quadrant. Set the tiles along the layout lines first, then fill in the interior tiles.

Note: Cut tile shown inverted for clarity; tiles should be faceup for marking.

4 Cut tiles to fit against the walls. First, lay the tile to be cut (A) on top of the last full tile you installed. Position a ⅛"-thick spacer against the wall, then set a marker tile (B) on top of the tile to be cut. The uncovered portion of the tile to be cut will be the part you install. Trace along the edge of the marker tile to draw a cutting line.

(continued next page)

Tip: To mark tiles for cutting around outside corners, first make a cardboard template to match the space, with a 1/8" gap along the walls. After cutting the template, check to make sure it fits. Place the template on a tile, and trace its outline.

5 Cut the tile to fit, using a straightedge and a utility knife. Hold the straightedge securely against cutting lines to ensure a straight cut.

Option: To score and cut thick vinyl tiles (and ceramic tiles), use a tile cutter (page 75).

6 Install cut tiles next to the walls. Tip: For efficiency, you can precut all tiles, but first measure the distance between the wall and installed tiles at various points to make sure the variation does not exceed ½".

7 Continue installing tile in the remaining working quadrants until the room is completely covered. Check the entire floor, and if you find loose areas, press down on the tiles to bond them to the underlayment. Install metal threshold bars at project borders where the new floor joins another floor covering (page 63).

How to Install Dry-back Tile

1 Begin applying adhesive around the intersection of the layout lines, using a trowel with 1/16" V-shaped notches. Hold the trowel at a 45° angle, and spread adhesive evenly over the surface.

2 Spread adhesive over most of the installation area, covering three quadrants. Allow the adhesive to set according to manufacturer's instructions, then begin to install the tile at the intersection of the layout lines. (You can kneel on installed tiles to lay additional tiles.) When one quadrant is completely tiled, spread adhesive over the remaining quadrants, then finish setting the tile.

Ceramic Tile

Ceramic tile includes a wide variety of hard flooring products made from molded clay. Although there are significant differences among the various types, they are all installed using cement-based mortar as an adhesive and grout to fill the gaps between tiles. These same techniques can be used to install tiles cut from natural stone, like granite and marble.

Tile is the hardest of all flooring materials. With few exceptions, it is also the most expensive. But its durability makes it well worth the extra cost.

To ensure a long-lasting tile installation, the underlayment must be solid. Cementboard (or the thinner fiber/cementboard) is the best underlayment, since it has excellent stability and resists moisture. However, in rooms where moisture is not a factor, plywood is an adequate underlayment, and is considerably cheaper.

Many ceramic tiles have a glazed surface that protects the porous clay from staining. Unglazed ceramic tile should be protected with a sealer after it is installed. Grout sealers will prevent grout joints from trapping dirt and becoming discolored.

This section shows:
- Choosing Tile for Your Floor (pages 72 to 73)
- Tools & Materials (pages 74 to 75)
- Cutting Tile (pages 76 to 77)
- Installing Ceramic Tile (pages 78 to 85)

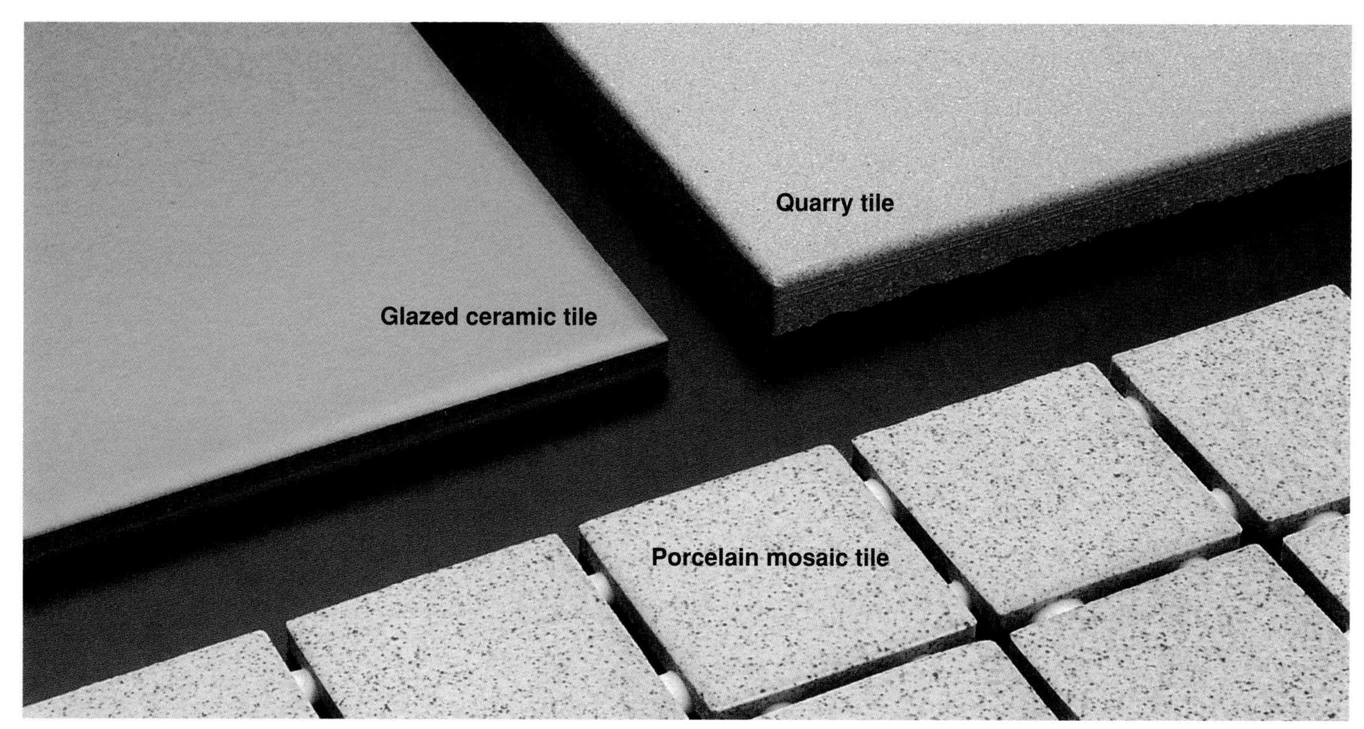

Ceramic tiles include several categories of products that are molded from clay, then baked in a kiln. *Glazed ceramic tile* is coated with a colored glaze after it is baked, then is fired again to produce a hard surface layer, which is clearly visible when the tile is viewed along the edges. *Quarry tile* is an unglazed, porous tile that is typically softer and thicker than glazed tiles. *Porcelain mosaic tile* is extremely dense and hard, and is naturally water-resistant. Like quarry tiles, porcelain tiles have the same color throughout their thickness when viewed along the edges. Porcelain tiles are often sold in mosaic sheets with a fiber or paper backing.

Natural-stone tiles are cut from stone extracted from quarries around the world. They are easily identified by visible saw marks at the edges and by their mineral veins or spots. Granite and marble tiles are generally sold with polished and sealed surfaces. Slate tiles are formed by cleaving the stone along natural faults, rather than by machine-cutting, giving the tiles an appealing, textured look. Stone tile can be prohibitively expensive for large installations, but can be used economically as an accent in highly visible areas.

Ceramic Tile

Choosing Tile for Your Floor

A quality tile installation can last for decades, so make sure to choose colors and designs that will have long-lasting appeal. Be wary of trendy styles that may look dated in few years.

The time and labor required to install and maintain tile can also influence your decision. Square tiles have fewer grout lines and are therefore easier to maintain.

Square tiles come in many sizes. Commonly available sizes range from 6" to 12". Larger tiles can be installed relatively quickly and require less maintenance; they can also make a room look larger.

Irregular tile shapes include rectangles, hexagons, and octagons. Spaces between irregular tiles are often filled with smaller diamond or square-shaped tiles.

Mosaic tiles come in unglazed porcelain and glazed ceramic varieties. They are held together and installed in sheets with paper gauze backing or plastic webbing. Mosaic tiles come in a variety of sizes and shapes, though the most common forms are 1" and 2" squares.

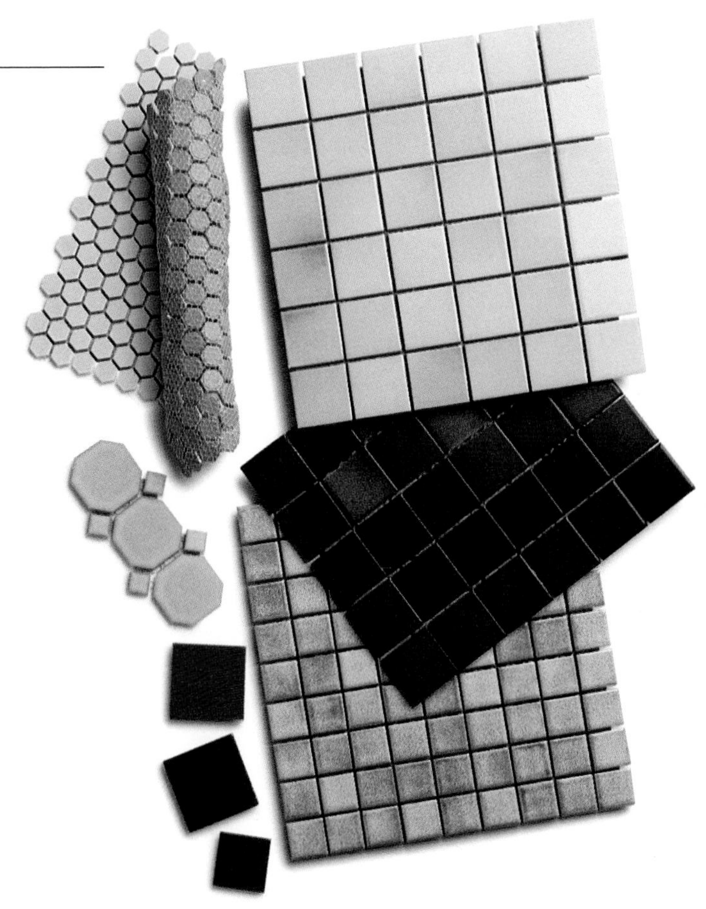

Accent tiles, including mosaic borders and printed glazed tiles, can be used as continuous borders or placed individually among the other tiles.

Thin-set mortar is a fine-grained cement product used to bond floor tile to underlayment. It is prepared by adding liquid a little at a time to the dry materials and stirring the mixture to achieve a creamy consistency. Some mortars include a latex additive in the dry mix, but with others you will need to add liquid latex additive when you prepare the mortar.

Ceramic Tile

Tools & Materials

The tools required to cut tiles and to apply mortar and grout are generally small and fairly inexpensive.

Materials needed for a tile installation include: adhesive thin-set mortar, used to fasten the tiles to the underlayment; grout, used to fill the joints between tiles; and sealers, used to protect the tile surface and grout lines. Make sure to use the materials recommended by the tile manufacturer.

Trim and finishing materials for tile installations include base-trim tiles (A) which fit around the room perimeter, and bullnose tiles (B) used at doorways and other transition areas. Doorway thresholds (C) are made from synthetic materials as well as natural materials, such as marble, and come in thicknesses ranging from ¼" to ¾" to match different floor levels.

Tiling tools include adhesive-spreading tools, cutting tools, and grouting tools. Notched trowels (A) for spreading mortar come with notches of varying sizes and shapes; the size of the notch should be proportional to the size of the tile being installed. Cutting tools include a tile cutter (B), tile nippers (C), handheld tile cutter (D), and jig saw with tungsten-carbide blade (E). Grouting tools include a grout float (F), grout sponge (G), buff rag (H), and foam brush (I). Other tiling tools include spacers (J), available in different sizes to create grout joints of varying widths; needlenose pliers (K) for removing spacers; rubber mallet (L) for setting tiles into mortar; and caulk gun (M).

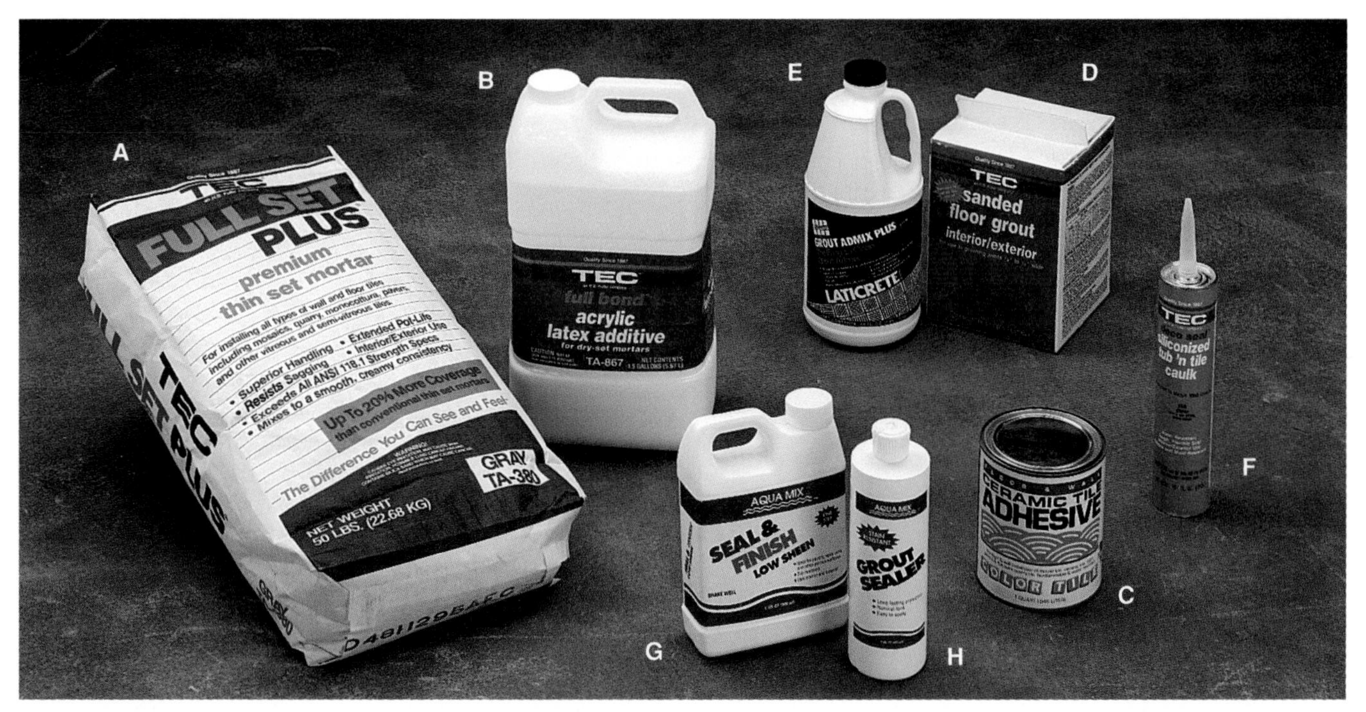

Tile materials include adhesives, grouts, and sealers. Thin-set mortar (A), the most common floor-tile adhesive, is often strengthened with latex mortar additive (B). Use wall-tile adhesive (C) for installing base-trim tile. Floor grout (D), is used to fill gaps between tiles; it is available in pretinted colors to match your tile. Grout can be made more resilient and durable with grout additive (E). Tile caulk (F) should be used in place of grout where tile meets another surface, like a bathtub. Porous tile sealer (G) and grout sealer (H) ward off stains and make maintenance easier.

Ceramic Tile

Cutting Tile

Cutting tile accurately takes some practice and patience, but can be done effectively by do-it-yourselfers with the right tools.

Most cutting can be done with a basic tile cutter, such as the one shown on the opposite page. Tile cutters come in various configurations; each operates a little differently, though they all score and snap tile. Tile stores will often lend cutters to customers.

Other hand-held cutting tools are used to make small cuts or curved cuts.

Everything You Need:

Tools: wet saw, tile cutter, hand-held tile cutter, nippers, jig saw with tungsten-carbide blade.

Tile saws—also called wet saws because they use water to cool blades and tiles—are used primarily for cutting natural-stone tiles. They are also useful for quickly cutting notches in all kinds of hard tile. Wet saws are available for rent at tile dealers and rental shops.

Tips for Making Special Cuts

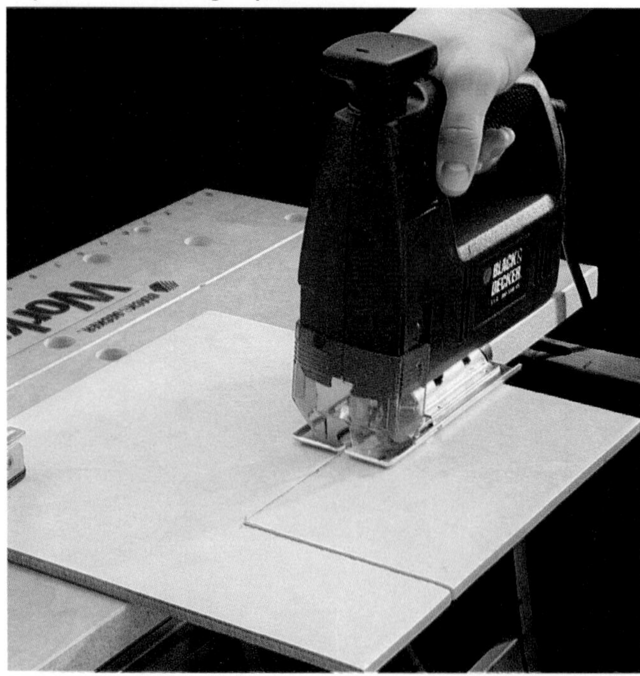

To make square notches, clamp the tile down on a worktable, then use a jig saw with a tungsten-carbide blade to make the cuts. If you need to cut many notches, a wet saw is more efficient.

To cut mosaic tiles, use a tile cutter to score tiles in the row where the cut will occur. Cut away excess strips of mosaics from the sheet, using a utility knife, then use a hand-held tile cutter to snap tiles one at a time. NOTE: Use tile nippers to cut narrow portions of tiles after scoring.

How to Make Straight Cuts in Ceramic Tile

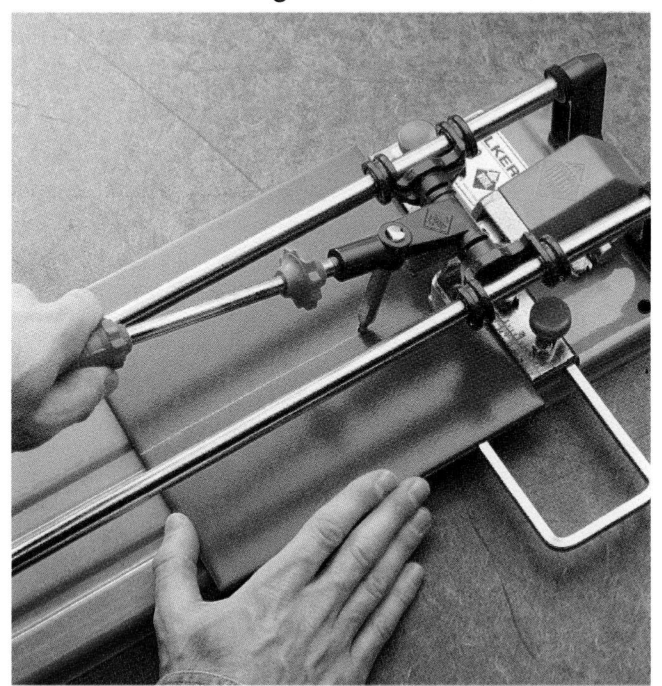

1 Mark a cutting line on the tile with a pencil, then place the tile in the cutter so the tile-cutting wheel is directly over the line. Pressing down firmly on the wheel handle, run the wheel across the tile to score the surface.

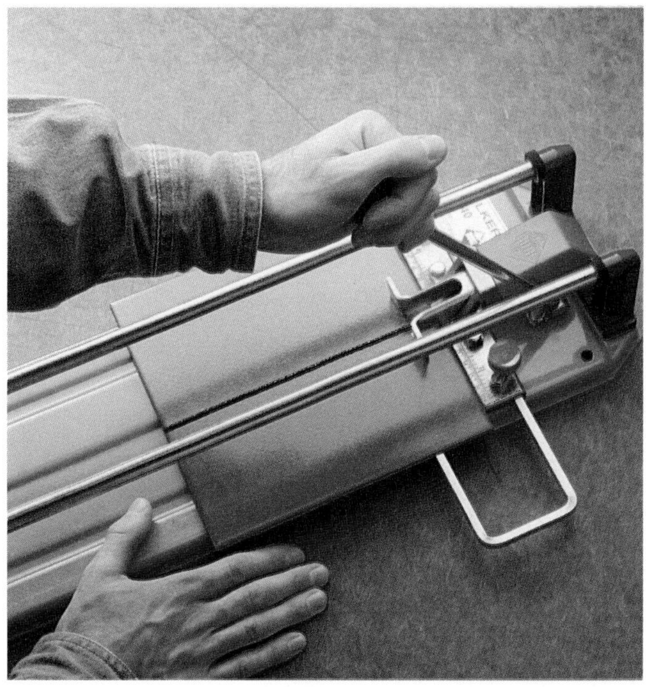

2 Snap the tile along the scored line, as directed by the tool manufacturer. Usually, snapping the tile is accomplished by depressing a lever on the tile cutter.

How to Make Curved Cuts with Tile Nippers

1 Mark a cutting line on the tile face, then use the scoring wheel of a hand-held tile cutter to score the cut line. Make several parallel scores, not more than ¼" apart, in the waste portion of the tile.

2 Use tile nippers to gradually remove the scored portion of the tile. TIP: To cut circular holes in the middle of a tile (step 9, page 81), first score and cut the tile so it divides the hole in two, using the straight-cut method, then use the curved-cut method to remove waste material from each half of the hole.

Installing Ceramic Tile

Ceramic tile installations start with the same steps as resilient tile projects: snapping perpendicular layout lines and dry-fitting tiles to ensure the best placement. These steps are shown on pages 64 to 66.

When you start setting tiles in thin-set mortar, work in small sections at a time so the mortar does not dry before the tiles are set. Also, plan your installation to avoid kneeling on set tiles.

Everything You Need:

Tools: basic hand tools (page 27), rubber mallet, tile cutter, tile nippers, hand-held tile cutter, needlenose pliers, grout float, grout sponge, soft cloth, small paint brush.

Materials: thin-set mortar, tile, tile spacers, grout, grout sealer, tile caulk.

How to Install Ceramic Tile

1 Draw reference and layout lines (pages 64 to 66), then mix a batch of thin-set mortar (page 74). Spread thin-set mortar evenly against both reference lines of one quadrant, using a ¼" square-notched trowel. Use the edge of the trowel to create furrows in the mortar bed.

VARIATION: For large tiles or uneven natural stone, use a larger trowel with notches that are at least ½" deep.

2 Set the first tile in the corner of the quadrant where the reference lines intersect. TIP: When setting tiles that are 8" square or larger, twist each tile slightly as you set it into position.

3 Using a soft rubber mallet, gently rap the central area of each tile a few times to set it evenly into the mortar.

VARIATION: For mosaic sheets, use a $\frac{3}{16}$" V-notched trowel to spread mortar, and use a grout float to press the sheets into the mortar.

4 To ensure consistent spacing between tiles, place plastic tile spacers at corners of the set tile. NOTE: With mosaic sheets, use spacers equal to the gaps between tiles.

(continued next page)

5 Position and set adjacent tiles into mortar along the reference lines. Make sure tiles fit neatly against the spacers. NOTE: Spacers are only temporary; be sure to remove them before the mortar hardens.

6 To make sure adjacent tiles are level with one another, lay a straight piece of 2 × 4 across several tiles at once, and rap the 2 × 4 with a mallet.

7 Lay tile in the remaining area covered with mortar. Repeat steps 1 to 6, continuing to work in small sections, until you reach walls or fixtures.

8 Measure and mark tiles for cutting to fit against walls and into corners (pages 67 to 68). Cut tiles to fit (pages 76 to 77). Apply thin-set mortar directly to the back of the cut tiles instead of the floor, using the notched edge of the trowel to furrow the mortar.

9 Set cut pieces into position, and press down on them until they are level with adjacent tiles.

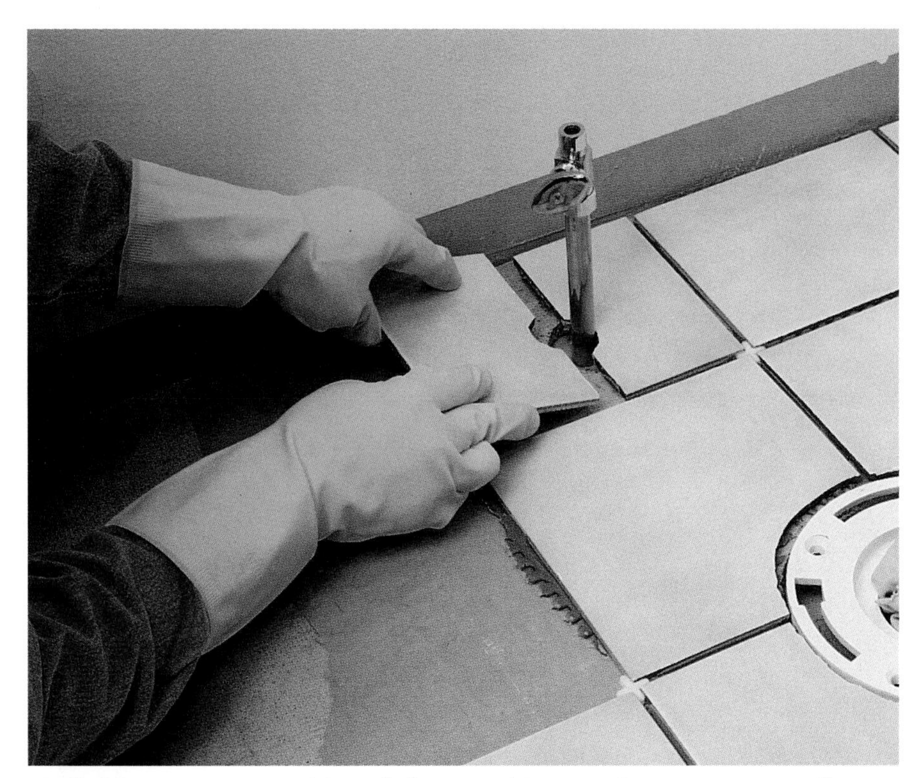

10 Measure, cut, and install tiles requiring notches or curves to fit around obstacles, such as exposed pipes or toilet drains.

11 Carefully remove spacers with needlenose pliers before the mortar hardens.

(continued next page)

12 Apply mortar and fill in tiles in remaining quadrants, completing one quadrant at a time before beginning the next. TIP: Before applying grout, inspect all of the tile joints and remove any high spots of mortar that could show through grout, using a utility knife or a grout knife.

13 Install threshold material in doorways. The most long-lasting thresholds are made from solid-surface mineral products. If the threshold is too long for the doorway, cut it to fit with a jig saw or circular saw and a tungsten-carbide blade. Set the threshold in thin-set mortar so the top is even with the tile. Keep the same space between the threshold as between tiles. Let the mortar cure for at least 24 hours.

14 Prepare a small batch of floor grout to fill tile joints. TIP: When mixing grout for porous tile, such as quarry or natural stone, use an additive with a release agent to prevent grout from bonding to the tile surfaces.

15 Starting in a corner, pour the grout over the tile. Use a rubber grout float to spread grout outward from the corner, pressing firmly on float to completely fill joints. For best results, tilt the float at a 60° angle to the floor and use a figure-eight motion.

16 Use the grout float to remove excess grout from the surface of the tile. Wipe diagonally across the joints, holding the float in a near-vertical position. Continue applying grout and wiping off excess until about 25 sq. ft. of the floor has been grouted.

17 Wipe a damp grout sponge diagonally over about 2 sq. ft. of the tile at a time to remove excess grout. Rinse the sponge in cool water between wipes. Wipe each area once only; repeated wiping can pull grout from the joints. Repeat steps 14 to 17 to apply grout to the rest of the floor.

18 Allow the grout to dry for about 4 hours, then use a soft cloth to buff the tile surface free of any remaining grout film.

(continued next page)

How to Install Ceramic Tile (continued)

19 Apply grout sealer to the grout lines, using a small sponge brush or sash brush. Avoid brushing sealer on the tile surfaces. Wipe up any excess sealer immediately.

VARIATION: Use a tile sealer to seal porous tile, such as quarry tile or any unglazed tile. Roll a thin coat of sealer (refer to manufacturer's instructions) over the tile and grout joints with a paint roller and extension handle.

How to Install Base-trim Tile

1 To give your new tiled floor a more professional look, install base-trim tiles at the bases of the walls. Start by dry-fitting the tiles to determine the best spacing (grout lines in base tile do not always align with grout lines in the floor tile). Use rounded "bullnose" tiles at outside corners, and mark tiles for cutting as needed.

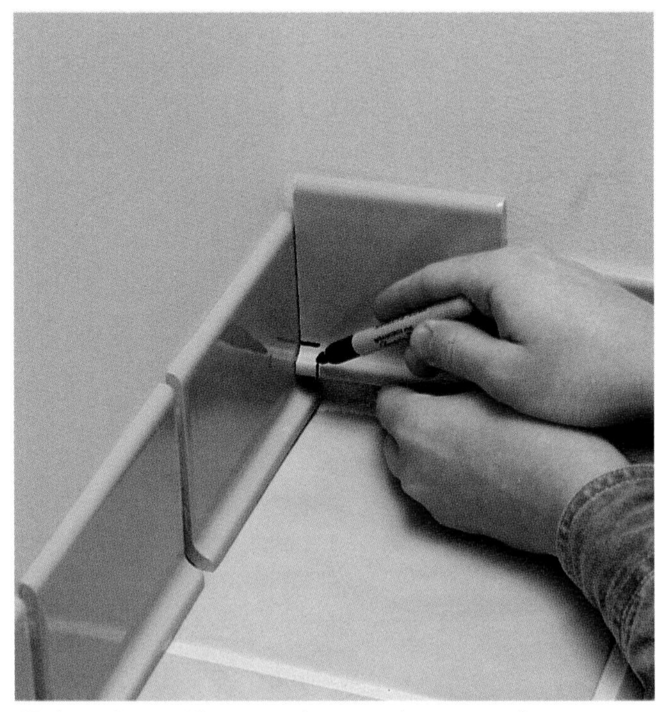

2 Leaving a 1/8" expansion gap between tiles at corners, mark any contour cuts necessary to allow the coved edges to fit together. Use a jig saw with a tungsten-carbide blade to make curved cuts (see page 76).

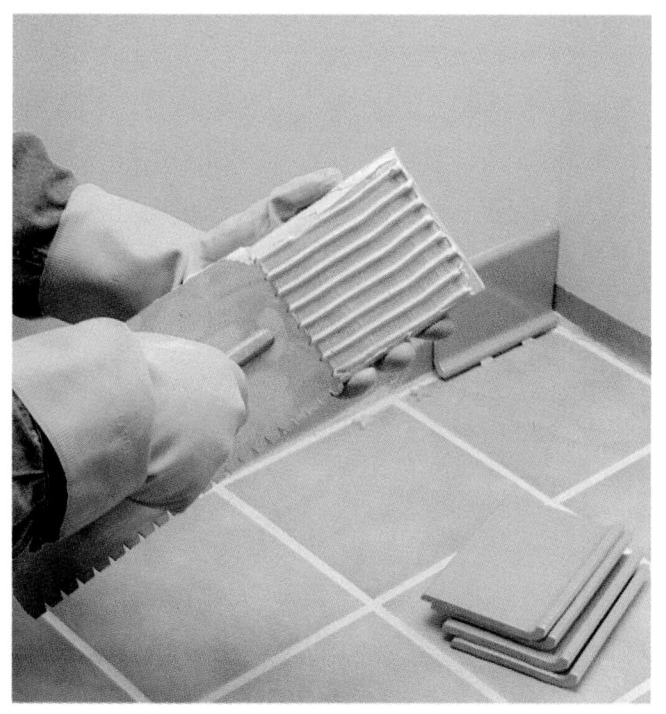

3 Begin installing base-trim tiles at an inside corner. Use a notched trowel to apply wall adhesive to the back of the tile. Slip ⅛" spacers under each tile to create an expansion joint.

4 Press the tile into the adhesive. Continue setting tiles, using spacers to maintain ⅛" gaps between the tiles and an expansion joint between the tile and the floor.

5 At outside corners, use a double-bullnose tile on one side, to cover the edge of the adjoining tile.

6 After adhesive dries, grout the vertical joints between tiles, and apply grout along the tops of the tiles to make a continuous grout line. After grout cures, fill the expansion joint at the bottom of the tiles with caulk.

A diagonal floor pattern is easy to install once you establish reference lines at a 45° angle to the original layout lines (step 3, page 65). Installation is similar to that of ordinary square tile, except that trim cuts will be diagonal.

Advanced Tile Techniques

Confident do-it-yourselfers familiar with basic tile techniques may be ready to undertake a project more challenging than a standard square tile floor installation. While the installations shown here usually require more time, the finished effect is well worth the extra effort.

For example, simply rotating the layout by 45° can yield striking results, as shown in the photo above. Offsetting the joints in adjacent tile rows to create a "running bond" pattern, a technique borrowed from masonry (opposite page), also adds visual interest. A third technique features a unique geometrical look using hexagonal tile. The final project shown, installing a tile border, employs a combination of techniques to create the look of an elegant area rug, using tile.

The four advanced tile projects shown in this section assume a basic knowledge of tile installation techniques (pages 76 to 85). For this reason, this section focuses on layout issues specific to certain tile shapes or desired effects.

How to Lay a Running-bond Tile Pattern

1 Start a running-bond tile installation by dry-fitting tile in the standard manner to establish working reference lines (page 66). Dry-fit a few tiles side by side, using spacers to maintain proper joint spacing, and measure the total width of the dry-fitted section (A). Use this measurement to snap a series of equally spaced parallel lines to help keep your installation straight. Running-bond layouts are most effective with rectangular tiles.

2 Spread thin-set mortar and lay the first row of tiles starting at a point where the layout lines intersect. Offset the next row by a measurement equal to one-half the length of the tile.

3 Continue setting tiles, filling one quadrant at a time, using the parallel reference lines as guides to keep the rows straight. Immediately wipe off any mortar that falls on the tiles. When finished, allow the mortar to cure, then follow the steps for grouting and cleaning (page 83).

How to Lay Hexagonal Tile

1 Snap perpendicular reference lines on the underlayment, then lay out three or four tiles in each direction along the layout lines, using plastic spacers with one flange between the tiles to maintain even spacing. Measure the length of this layout in both directions (A, B). Use measurement A to snap a series of equally spaced parallel lines across the entire floor, then do the same for measurement B in the other direction.

2 Apply dry-set mortar and begin setting tile as with square tile (pages 78 to 84). Apply mortar directly to the undersides of any tiles that extend outside the mortar bed.

3 Continue setting tiles, using the grid layout and spacers to keep your work aligned. Wipe off any mortar that falls on the tile surfaces. When finished, allow the mortar to cure, then follow the steps for applying grout (pages 82 to 84).

How to Lay a Tile Border with a Diagonal Pattern

1 Snap perpendicular reference lines, then dry-fit border tiles in the planned area, using spacers. Make sure the border tiles are aligned with the reference lines. Next, dry-fit the tiles at the outside corners of the border arrangement. Adjust the tile positions to create a layout with minimal cutting (this will take some trial-and-error). When the layout of the tiles is set, snap chalk lines around the border tiles and trace the edges of the outside tiles. Install these tiles.

2 Install the field tiles inside the tile border. For an interesting visual effect, draw layout lines that are at a 45° angle from the perpendicular reference lines to create diagonal layout lines.

3 Use standard tile-setting techniques to fill in the field tiles in the inside border (pages 78 to 84, and 86). TIP: Kneel on a wide board to distribute your weight if you need to work in a tiled area that has not cured overnight.

Installing manufactured wood flooring materials is a quicker, easier process than laying traditional solid hardwood. The hardwood veneer product shown here is edge-glued, using ordinary wood glue.

Hardwood Flooring

Hardwood flooring has undeniable appeal, but installing traditional solid hardwood planks is an expensive, difficult, and time-consuming job that few do-it-yourselfers are willing to attempt. However, many manufactured wood flooring products, designed for do-it-yourself installation, are now available. These materials offer the virtues of solid hardwood—strength; durability; attractive, warm appearance—but are easier to install.

These composite products come already stained and sealed with a protective coating. Like their solid hardwood counterparts, manufactured products have tongue-and-groove construction that ensures a tight bond between pieces.

Laminated planks can be installed in one of two ways. Flooring installed on a thin layer of adhesive is a good choice for areas that get a lot of foot traffic. A floating hardwood floor, which rests on a thin foam padding, can be installed over a variety of surfaces. It is the ideal choice over concrete slabs susceptible to moisture, such as those in basements.

Parquet flooring is installed with flooring adhesive, using the same installation strategy used for installing resilient or ceramic tile (pages 64 to 66).

Wood Flooring Options

Manufactured wood flooring materials include: fiberboard surfaced with a synthetic laminate layer that mimics the look of wood grain (left), plywood topped with a thin hardwood veneer (center), and parquet tiles made of wood strips bonded together in a decorative pattern (right).

Solid hardwood flooring is more expensive and more difficult to install than manufactured wood flooring. If you want a solid hardwood floor, consider hiring a professional to install it.

Stripping and refinishing an existing solid hardwood floor will give you a surface that looks like new. For help doing this, see our Black & Decker® Home Improvement Library™: *Refinishing & Finishing Wood.*

Materials for Hardwood Flooring Installation

Foam backing for use under floating plank floors comes in several thicknesses. The thinner foam backing on the left is installed under synthetic laminate flooring; the thicker backing on the right is laid under plywood-backed flooring.

Adhesives used to install hardwood flooring include white glue for joining edges of floating plank flooring and latex adhesive for glue-down floors.

T-shaped hardwood threshold spans transitions between hardwood floors and other flooring of equal height. These products, available through hardwood flooring manufacturers, are glued in place.

Reducers are wood transitions used between hardwood flooring and an adjacent floor of lower height. One edge is grooved to fit the tongue on hardwood planks, and the other edge has a rounded bullnose. Reducers come in several thicknesses and styles for your particular needs.

How to Cut Hardwood Flooring

Ripcut hardwood planks from the back side to avoid splintering the top surface when cutting. Measure the distance from the wall to the edge of the last board installed, subtracting ½" to allow for an expansion gap. Transfer the measurement to the back of the flooring, and mark the cut with a chalk line (left).

When ripcutting hardwood flooring with a circular saw, place another piece of flooring next to the piece marked for cutting to provide a stable surface for the foot of the saw (right). Also, clamp a cutting guide to the planks at the correct distance from the cutting line to ensure a straight cut.

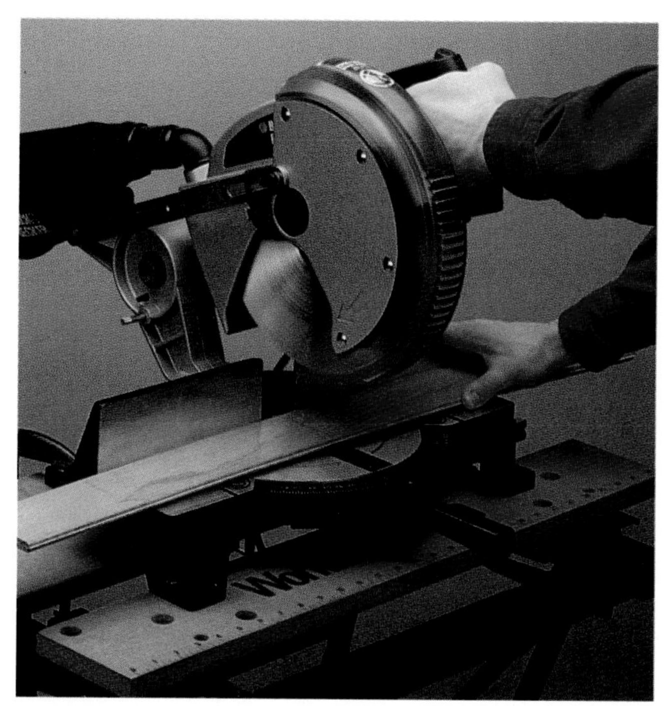

Crosscut hardwood planks on a power miter box, with the top surface of the planks facing up to prevent splintering.

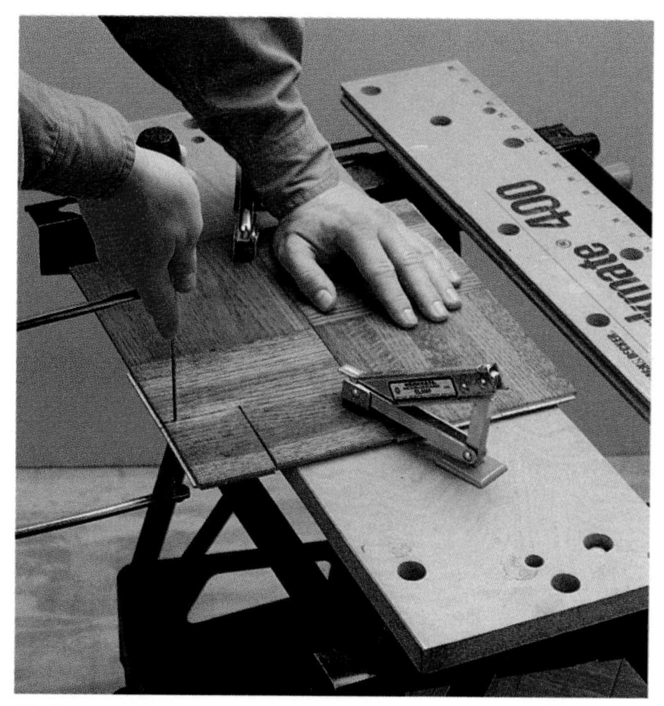

Make notched or curved cuts in hardwood flooring with a coping saw or jig saw. If using a jig saw, the finished surface of the flooring should face down.

Installing Hardwood Floors

How you install hardwood floors will depend on the product you have chosen. Synthetic laminate flooring should be installed only using the "floating" technique, in which the flooring is glued edge to edge and installed over a foam backing. Parquet flooring should only be glued down over troweled-on adhesive. Follow the instructions for "Installing Resilient Tile" (pages 64 to 66). Plywood-backed hardwood flooring can be installed using either method.

Everything You Need:

Tools: basic hand tools (page 27), coping saw, circular saw, ⅛" notched trowel, tool bar, mallet, linoleum roller.

Materials: hardwood flooring, flooring adhesive, wood glue, cardboard, foam backing, masking tape.

How to Install Wood Strip Flooring Using Adhesive

1 To establish a straight layout line, snap a chalk line parallel to the longest wall, about 30" from the wall. Kneel in this space to begin flooring installation.

2 Apply flooring adhesive to the subfloor on the other side of the layout line with a notched trowel, according to the manufacturer's directions. Take care not to obscure the layout line with adhesive.

3 Apply wood glue to the grooved end of each piece as you install it, to help joints stay tight. Do not apply glue to long sides of boards.

4 Install the first row of flooring with the edge of the tongues directly over chalk line. Make sure end joints are tight, then wipe up any excess glue immediately. At walls, leave a ½" space to allow for expansion of the wood. This gap will be covered by the baseboard and base shoe.

5 For succeeding rows, insert the tongue into the groove of the preceding row, and pivot the flooring down into the adhesive. Gently slide the tongue-and-groove ends together. TIP: At walls, you can use a hammer and a hardwood flooring tool bar to draw together the joints on the last strip (inset).

(continued next page)

6 After you've installed three or four rows, use a mallet and a scrap of flooring to gently tap boards together, closing up the seams. All joints should fit tightly.

7 Use a cardboard template to fit boards in irregular areas. Cut cardboard to match the space, and allow for a ½" expansion gap next to the wall. Trace the template outline on a board, then cut it to fit, using a jig saw. Finish layering strips over the entire floor.

8 Bond the flooring by rolling with a heavy flooring roller. Roll the flooring within 3 hours of the adhesive application. (Rollers can be borrowed or rented from flooring distributors.)

How to Install a Floating Plank Floor

1 Roll out the appropriate foam backing (page 92) and cut it in strips to fit the room. Secure all seams with masking tape. Do not overlap seams.

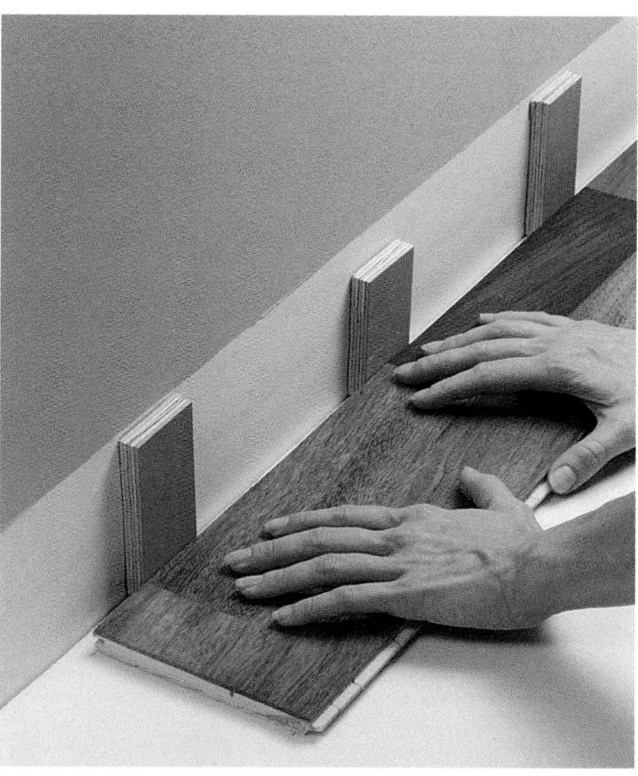

2 Begin installation at the longest wall. Use ½" spacers to provide a gap for expansion of the flooring.

3 Join planks by applying wood glue to the grooves of the planks. Complete the installation, using the same method used for glue-down flooring (steps 5 to 7). Be sure to glue end joints as well.

ROBERTS

Installing Carpet

Tackless strips and carpet bars secure carpeting at the edges of a room. Before it is secured, carpet is stretched with special tools so it is taut and lies flat.

Installing Carpet

For beginners, laying carpet can be a time-consuming job, but as you gain confidence using the specialty tools and techniques, the work becomes much easier. Carefully read the directions on the following pages before you begin, and, if possible, practice your skills on pieces of scrap carpet.

Careful planning and layout is crucial to a good, efficient carpet installation. In larger rooms, where you may need to join several pieces of carpet together, the proper layout can ensure that the seams will be invisible to the eye. Most installations will require that you stretch the carpet with specialty tools, using a carefully planned stretching sequence.

Have a helper on hand for the first stages of the project, when you will be moving the heavy rolls of padding and carpet into position and cutting them. Once the carpet is roughly in place, you can easily finish the project on your own.

This section shows:

Installing Carpet: A Step-by-Step Overview

1 Install transition materials (pages 110 to 111), then install tackless strips and padding around the perimeter of the room to secure the carpeting (page 112). Roll out carpet padding, and cut to fit (page 113).

2 Roll out and cut the carpet to fit, then join pieces with hot-glue seam tape, where necessary (pages 114 to 119).

3 Use a power stretcher and knee kicker to stretch the carpet and attach it around the perimeter of the room (pages 120 to 122).

4 Trim the edges of the carpet, and secure them to the tackless strips (page 123).

Read labels on the back of samples to learn useful technical information about the carpet. Labels usually tell you what material was used for the carpet fibers, the available widths (usually 12 or 15 feet), what anti-stain treatments were applied, and details of the product warranty.

Buying & Estimating Carpet

When choosing carpet for your home, you need to consider more than just color and pattern. The material used in the carpet can affect its durability: in high-traffic areas, such as hallways, choosing a top-quality fiber will result in longer wear. The construction of the carpet—the way in which the fibers are attached to the backing—can affect both its durability and its appearance. Even the width of the roll can influence your decision. If you're carpeting a 14-foot-wide room, for example, you may want to choose a carpet available in 15-foot-wide rolls to eliminate the need for seaming.

When seaming is unavoidable, calculate the total square footage to be covered, then add an additional 20% to ensure that you will be able to trim and seam the carpet correctly.

Tips for Evaluating Carpet

Examine the carpet backing, or foundation. A tighter grid pattern in the backing (top) usually indicates dense-pile carpet that will be more durable and soil-resistant than carpet with looser pile (bottom).

Fiber Type	Characteristics
Nylon	Easy to clean, very durable, good stain resistance; colors sometimes fade in direct sunlight.
Polyester	Excellent stain resistance, very soft in thick cut-pile constructions; colors don't fade in sunlight.
Olefin	Virtually stain- and fadeproof, resists moisture and static; not as resilient as nylon or as soft as polyester.
Acrylic	Resembles wool in softness and look, good moisture resistance; less durable than other synthetics.
Wool	Luxurious look and feel, good durability and warmth; more costly and less stain-resistant than synthetics.

Consider fiber composition when selecting a carpet, and choose materials with characteristics that are suited for your installation.

Carpet Construction

The top surface of a carpet, called the pile, consists of yarn loops pushed up through a backing material. The loops are left intact or cut by the manufacturer, depending on the desired effect. Most carpet sold today is made from synthetic fibers, such as nylon, polyester, and olefin, although natural wool carpet is still popular.

A good rule of thumb for judging the quality of a carpet is to look at the pile density. A carpet with more pile fibers packed into a given area will resist crushing, will be better at repelling stains and dirt buildup, and will be more durable than an inexpensive carpet with low pile density.

Cushion-backed carpet has a foam backing bonded to it, eliminating the need for additional padding. Cushion-backed carpet is easy to install, because it requires no stretching or tackless strips. Instead, it is secured with general-purpose adhesive, much like full-spread sheet vinyl (page 63). Cushion-backed carpet usually costs less than conventional carpet, but it is generally a lower-quality product.

Loop-pile carpet has a textured look, created by the rounded ends of the uncut yarn loops pushed up through the backing. The loops can be arranged randomly, or they can make a distinct pattern, such as herringbone. Loop-pile is ideal for heavy-traffic areas, since loops are virtually impervious to crushing.

Velvet cut-pile carpet has the densest pile of any carpet type. It is cut so that the color remains uniform when the pile is brushed in any direction. Velvets are well suited to formal living spaces.

Saxony cut-pile carpet, also known as *plush*, is constructed to withstand crushing and matting better than velvets. The pile is trimmed at a bevel, giving it a speckled appearance.

Carpet Planning & Layout Tips

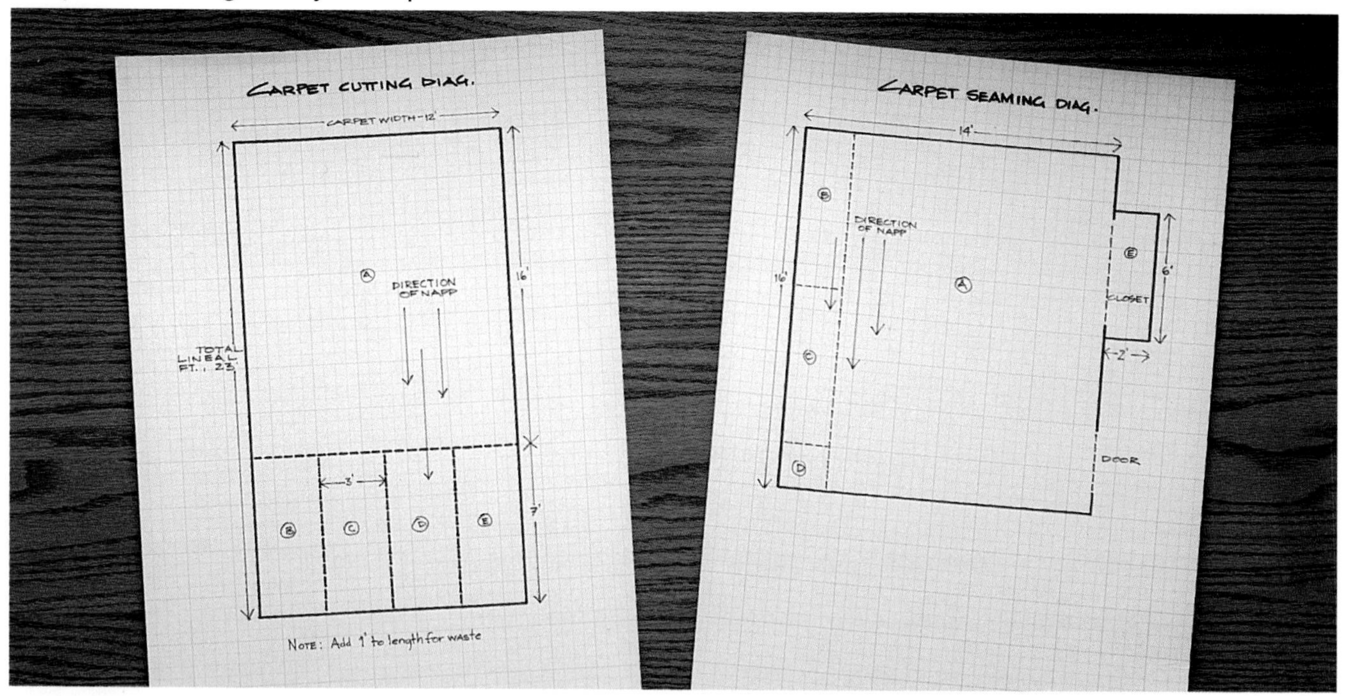

Sketch a scale drawing of the factory carpet roll and another drawing of the room to be carpeted. Use the drawings to plan cuts and show how the carpet pieces will be arranged. In most large rooms, the installation will include one large piece of carpet the same width as the factory roll, and several smaller pieces, which are permanently seamed to the larger piece. Follow the tips shown on this page when sketching the layout; remember that carpet pieces must be oversized to allow for precise seaming and trimming. Your finished drawings will tell you the length of carpet you need to buy.

Keep pile direction consistent. Carpet pile is usually slanted; this affects how the carpet looks from different angles, as light reflects off the surface. Orient seamed pieces so pile faces the same way.

Maintain patterns when seaming patterned carpet. Because of this, there is always more waste when installing patterned carpet. For a pattern that repeats every 18", for example, each piece must be oversized by 18" to ensure that the pattern is aligned. Pattern repeat measurements are noted on carpet samples.

At seams, add an extra 3" to each piece to provide the necessary surplus for cutting straight seam edges.

At each wall, add 6" to each carpet piece.This surplus will be trimmed away when the carpet is cut to the exact size of the room.

Closet floors usually are covered with a separate piece of carpet that is seamed to the room carpet.

For stairs, first find the length of carpet needed by adding together the rise and run of each step. Next, measure the width of the stairway to determine how many strips you can cut from the factory roll. For a 3-ft.-wide stairway, for example, you can cut three strips from a 12-ft.-wide roll, allowing for waste. Rather than seaming carpet strips together end to end, plan the installation so the ends of the strips fall in the stair crotches.

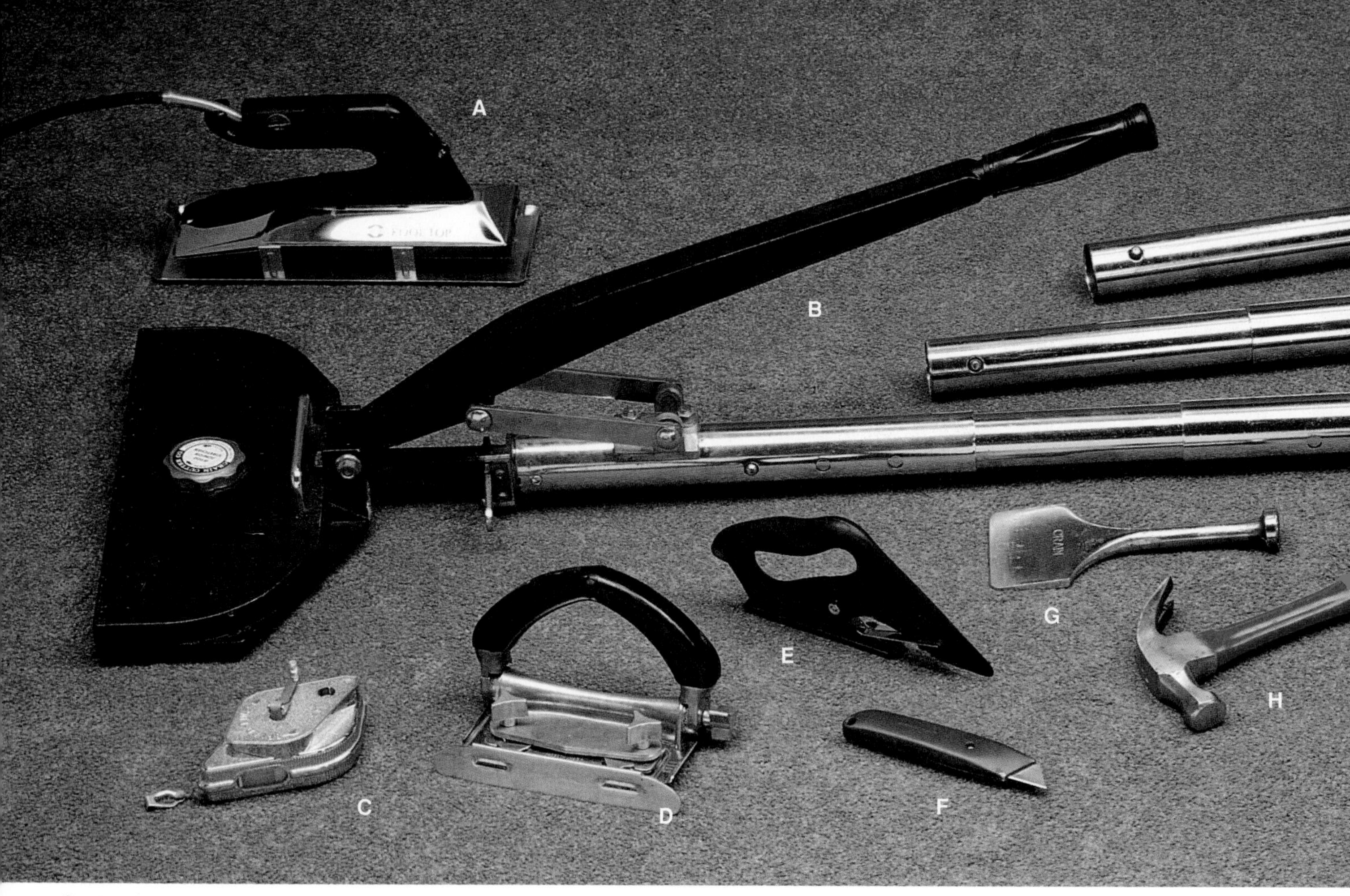

Carpeting tools include: seam iron (A), power stretcher and extensions (B), chalk line (C), edge trimmer (D), row-running knife (E), utility knife (F), stair tool (G), hammer (H), knee kicker (I), snips (J), scissors (K), and stapler (L).

Tools & Materials

Installing carpet requires the use of some specialty tools, most notably the knee kicker and power stretcher. These tools are available at most rental shops.

Other than the carpet itself, the pad is the most important material in a carpet installation. In addition to making your carpet feel more plush underfoot, the pad makes your floor quieter and warmer. And by cushioning the carpet fibers, the pad reduces wear and extends the life of your carpet. Especially if you are installing expensive carpet, use the best padding you can afford.

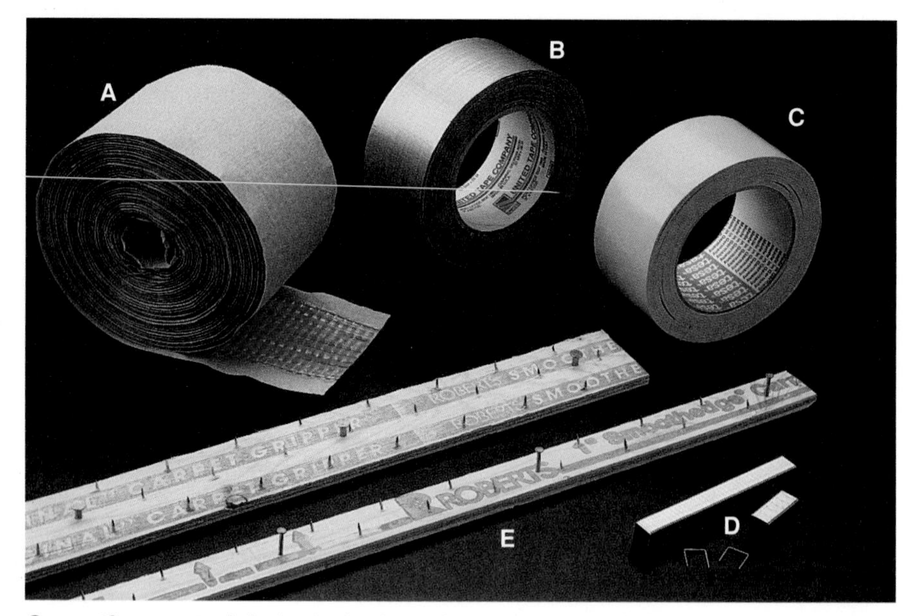

Carpeting materials include: hot-glue seam tape (A), used to join carpet pieces together; duct tape (B), for seaming carpet pads; double-sided tape (C), used to secure a carpet pad to concrete; staples (D), used to fasten padding to underlayment; and tackless strips (E), for securing the edges of stretched carpet.

Carpet padding comes in several varieties, including: bonded urethane foam (A), cellular sponge rubber (B), grafted prime foam (C), and prime urethane (D). Inexpensive bonded urethane padding is sufficient for low-traffic areas. Prime urethane and grafted prime foam are good for high-traffic areas, but are not suited for use with berbers or other stiff-backed carpets; for these, use ⅜"-thick bonded urethane foam or cellular sponge rubber. Foam padding is categorized according to thickness and density, measured in pounds per cubic foot; the denser the foam, the better the pad. Rubber padding is sold according to ounce-weight per square yard; the heavier the weight, the better the pad.

A knee kicker has teeth that grab the foundation of the carpet, then stretch it forward when the operator's knee is thrust against the cushioned back. Knee kickers are useful in tight areas.

Tools & Materials

Using a Knee Kicker & Power Stretcher

The most important tools for installing carpet are the knee kicker and power stretcher, which are used to stretch a carpet smooth and taut before securing it to tackless strips installed around the perimeter of a room.

The power stretcher is the more efficient of the two tools, and should be used to stretch and secure as much of the carpet as possible. The knee kicker is used to secure carpet in tight areas where the power stretcher cannot reach, such as closets.

A logical stretching sequence is essential to a good carpet installation. Begin attaching the carpet at a doorway or corner, then use the power stretcher and knee kicker to gradually stretch the carpet away from attached areas and toward the opposite walls.

How to Use a Knee Kicker

1 Adjust the depth of the gripping teeth by turning the knob on the knee kicker head. The teeth should be set deeply enough to grab the carpet foundation without penetrating through to the padding.

2 Place the kicker head a few inches away from the wall to avoid dislodging tackless strips, then strike the kicker cushion sharply with your knee, stretching the carpet taut. Tack the carpet to the pins on the tackless strips to hold it in place.

How to Assemble & Use a Power Stretcher

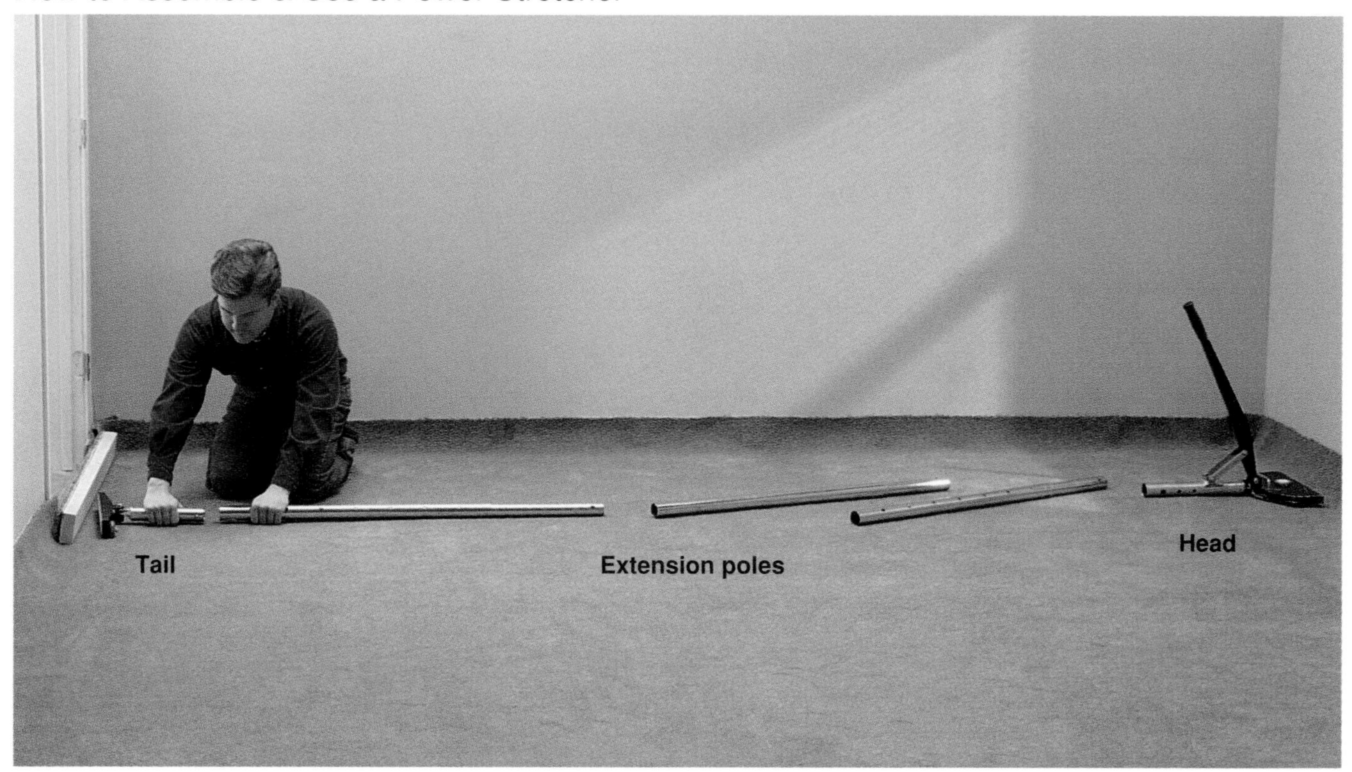

1 Align the pieces of the power stretcher along the floor, with the tail positioned at a point where the carpet is already secured, and the head positioned just short of the opposite wall. Fit the ends of the sections together.

2 Telescope one or more of the extensions until the tail rests against the starting wall and the head is about 5" from the wall on the opposite side of the room. Adjust the teeth on the head so they grip the carpet (step 1, previous page).

3 Depress the lever on the head of the stretcher to stretch the carpet. The stretcher head should move the carpet about 2".

Installing Carpet Transitions

Metal carpet bar

Tackless strip tuck-under

Hot-glue seam tape

Hardwood threshold

Doorways and other transitional areas require special treatment when you are installing carpet. Transition materials and techniques vary, depending on the level and type of the adjoining flooring (left).

For a transition to a floor that is either at the same height or lower than the bottom of the carpet, attach a metal carpet bar to the floor and secure the carpet inside the bar. This transition is often used where carpet meets a vinyl or tile floor. Carpet bars are sold in standard door-width lengths, and in longer strips.

For a transition to a floor that is higher than the carpet bottom, use tackless strips, as if the adjoining floor surface were a wall. This transition is common where carpet meets a hardwood floor.

For a transition to another carpet of the same height, join the two carpet sections with hot-glue seam tape (pages 118 to 119).

For a transition in a doorway between carpets of different heights or textures, install tackless strips and a hardwood threshold. Thresholds are available predrilled and ready to install with screws.

Everything You Need:

Tools: basic hand tools (page 27), knee kicker, stair tool.

Materials: transition materials.

How to Make Transitions with Metal Carpet Bars

1 Measure and cut a carpet bar to fit the space, then nail it in place. In doorways, the upturned metal flange should lie directly below the center of the door when closed. To install a carpet bar on concrete, see page 112.

2 Roll out, cut, and seam the carpet. Fold the carpet back in the transition area, then mark it for trimming—the edge of the carpet should fall ⅛" to ¼" short of the corner of the carpet bar so it can be stretched into the bar.

3 Use a knee kicker to stretch the carpet snugly into the corner of the carpet bar. Press the carpet down onto the pins with a stair tool. Then, bend the carpet bar flange down over the carpet by striking with a hammer and a block of wood.

How to Make Transitions with Tackless Strips

1 Install a tackless strip, leaving a gap equal to ⅔ the thickness of the carpet for trimming. Roll out, cut, and seam the carpet. Mark the edges of the carpet between the strip and the adjoining floor surface about ⅛" past the point where it meets the adjacent floor.

2 Use a straightedge and a utility knife to trim off the excess carpet. Stretch the carpet toward the strip with a knee kicker, then press it onto the pins of the strip.

3 Tuck the edge of the carpet into the gap between the tackless strip and the existing floor, using a stair tool.

Install tackless strips next to walls, leaving a gap equal to about ⅔ the thickness of the carpet. Make sure the angled pins on the tackless strips point toward the walls. Cut and install padding so it fits snugly against the strips. Many carpet pads have one side that is covered with a smooth coating. For information on selecting carpet padding, see page 107.

Installing Padding & Tackless Strips

The easiest way to secure carpeting is to install tackless strips around the perimeter of the room. Once the strips are installed, carpet padding is rolled out as a foundation for the carpet.

Standard ¾"-wide tackless strips are adequate for securing most carpet. For carpets laid on concrete, use wider tackless strips that are attached with masonry nails. Be careful when handling tackless strips—the sharp pins can be dangerous. Where the carpet will meet a doorway or another type of flooring, install the appropriate transitions (page 110).

Everything You Need:

Tools: basic hand tools (page 27), stapler, metal snips.

Materials: tackless strips (or double-sided tape, for concrete), carpet pad, duct tape.

How to Install Tackless Strips

1 Starting in a corner, nail tackless strips to the floor, maintaining a slight gap between the strips and the walls (see photo above). Use a scrap of plywood or cardboard as a spacing aid.

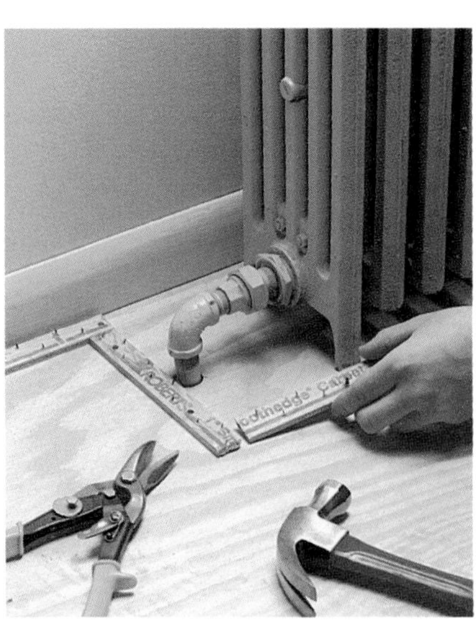

2 Use metal snips to cut the tackless strips to fit around radiators, door moldings, and other obstacles.

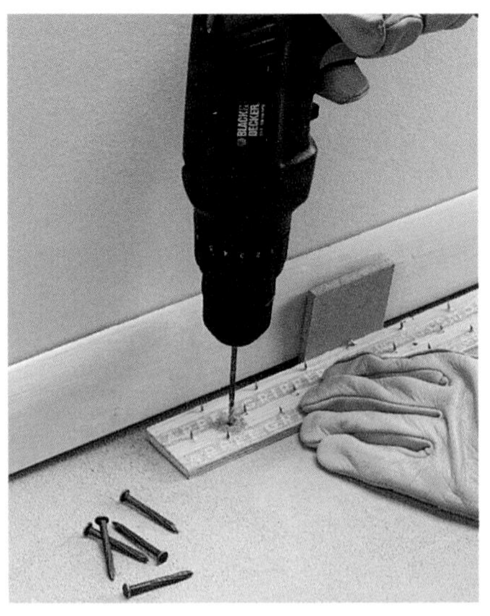

Variation: On concrete, use wider tackless strips. Drill pilot holes through the strips and into the floor, using a masonry bit, then fasten the strips by driving 1½" fluted masonry nails.

How To Install Carpet Padding

1 Roll out enough padding to cover the entire floor. Make sure seams between the strips are tight. If one face of the padding has a slicker surface, make sure the slick face is up. This makes it easier to slide the carpet over the pad during installation.

2 Use a utility knife to cut away any excess padding along edges. The padding should touch, but not overlap, the tackless strips.

3 Tape the seams together with duct tape, then staple the padding to the floor at 1-ft. intervals.

VARIATION: To fasten carpet padding to a concrete floor, apply double-sided tape next to the tackless strips and in an "X" pattern across the floor.

Installing Carpet

When laying carpeting, proper stretching technique is the key to a quality installation. Take the time to learn the techniques shown on pages 120 to 123, then plan the stretching sequence that will work best for your room.

For a one-piece carpet installation in a room narrower than your carpet roll, it is usually easiest to roll out the carpet in a more spacious area, such as in a basement or on a driveway, then loosely fold it lengthwise to move it into the project area. If you are installing carpet in a large room where seams are necessary, try to position seams so they are in low-traffic areas.

Mistakes can be expensive when laying carpet. If you do not have experience working with carpet, it is a good idea to practice seaming, stretching, and trimming techniques on scrap carpet before installing your new carpet.

The following pages demonstrate installation of standard wall-to-wall carpet. Cushion-back carpet is cut and seamed in much the same way, but it is not stretched and it does not require tackless strips. Instead, cushion-back carpet is laid using full-bond adhesives (page 63).

Everything You Need:

Tools: basic hand tools (page 27), knee kicker, stair tool, power stretcher, stapler, wall trimmer, carpet iron.

Materials: carpet, tackless strips, carpet bar, seam tape, seam glue.

How to Cut & Seam Carpet

1 Position the carpet roll against one wall, with its loose end extending up the wall by about 6", then roll out the carpet until it reaches the opposite wall.

2 At the opposite wall, mark the back of the carpet at each edge, about 6" up from where the carpet touches the wall. Pull the carpet back away from the wall, so the marks are visible.

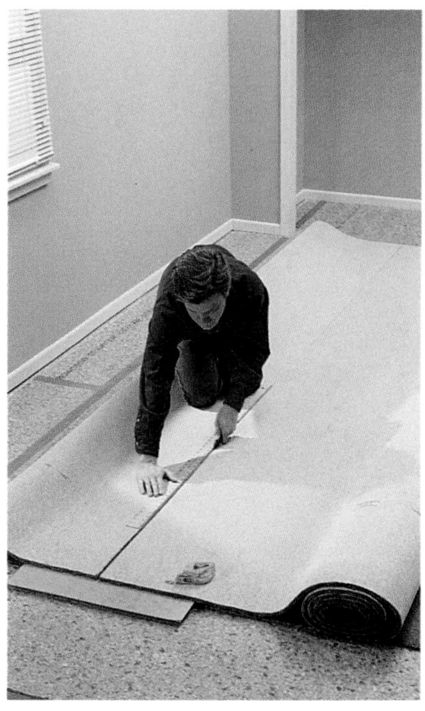

3 Snap a chalk line across the back of the carpet between the marks, then cut along the line, using a straightedge and utility knife. Place a piece of scrap plywood under the cutting area to protect the carpet and padding from the knife.

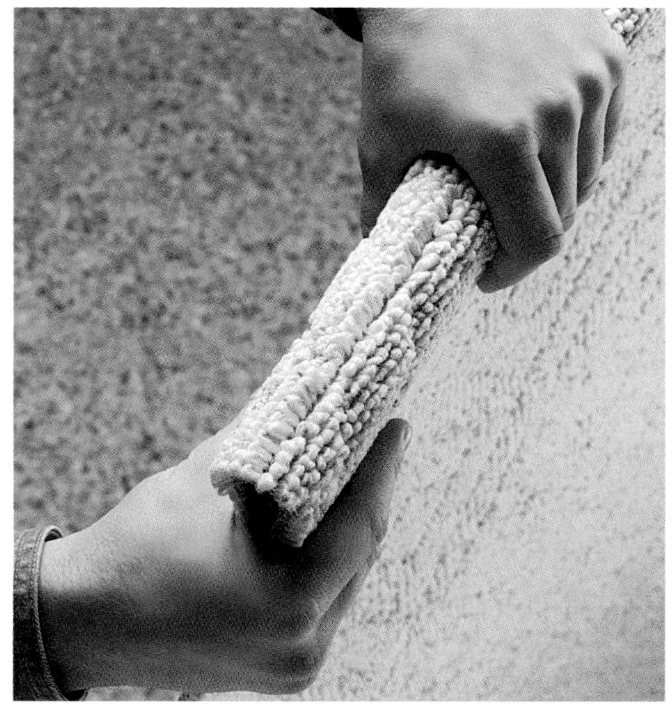

VARIATION: When cutting loop-pile carpet, avoid severing the loops by cutting from the top side, using a row-running knife (a specialty carpentry tool sold at carpet stores). First fold the carpet back along the cutline to part the pile (left). Make a crease along the part line. Then, lay the carpet flat and cut along the part in the pile (right). Cut slowly to ensure a straight cut.

(continued next page)

How to Cut & Seam Carpet (continued)

4 Next to walls, straddle the edge of the carpet and nudge it with your foot until it extends up the wall by about 6", and is parallel to the wall.

5 At the corners, relieve buckling by slitting the carpet with a utility knife, allowing the carpet to lie flat. Do not cut too far into the carpet.

6 Using your seaming plan (page 104) as a guide, measure and cut fill-in pieces of carpet to complete the installation. Be sure to include a 6" surplus at each wall and a 3" surplus on each edge that will be seamed to another piece of carpet. Set the cut pieces in place, making sure the pile faces in the same direction on all pieces.

7 Roll back the large piece of carpet on the side to be seamed, then use a chalk line to snap a straight seam edge, about 2" in from the factory edge. Keep the ends of the line about 1½ ft. in from the ends of the carpet, where the overlap onto the walls causes it to buckle.

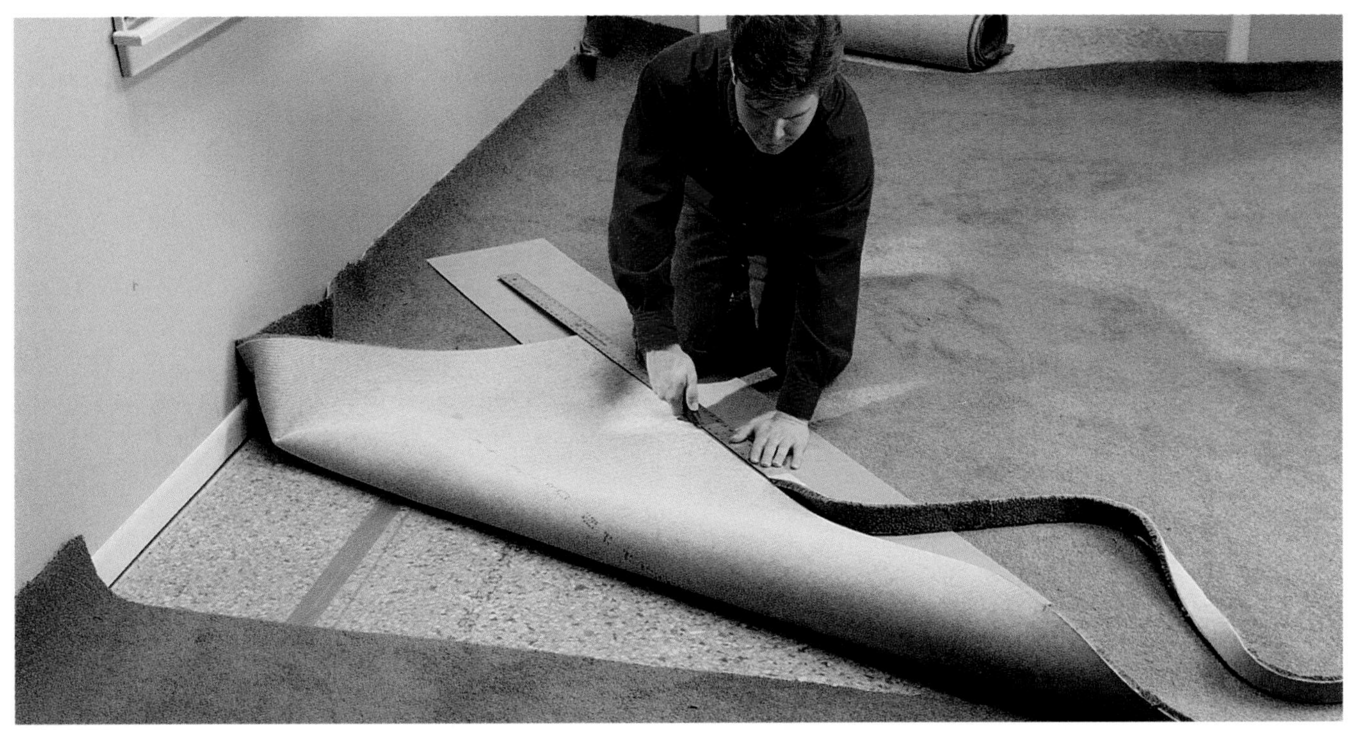

8 Using a straightedge and utility knife, carefully cut the carpet along the chalk line. To extend the cutting lines to the edges of the carpet, pull the corners back at an angle so they lie flat, then cut with the straightedge and utility knife. Place scrap wood under the cutting area to protect the carpet while cutting.

9 On the smaller carpet pieces, cut straight seam edges where the small pieces will be joined to one another. Do not cut the edges that will be seamed to the large carpet piece until after the small pieces are joined together.

Option: Apply a continuous bead of seam glue along the cut edges of the backing at seams to ensure that the carpet will not fray.

(continued next page)

10 Plug in the seam iron and set it aside to heat up, then measure and cut hot-glue seam tape for all seams. Begin by joining the small fill-in pieces to form one larger piece. Center the seam tape under a seam, with the adhesive side facing up.

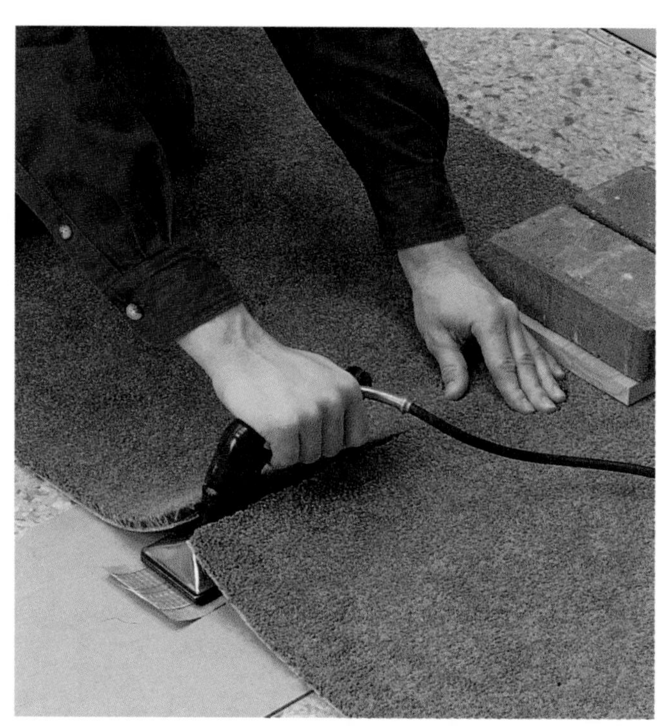

11 Set the iron under the carpet pieces at one end of the tape until the adhesive liquifies—usually about 30 seconds. Working in 12" sections, slowly move the iron along the tape, letting the carpet fall onto the hot adhesive behind it. Set weights at the end of the seam to hold the pieces in place.

12 Press the edges of the carpet together into the melted adhesive behind the iron. Separate the pile with your fingers to make sure no fibers are stuck in the glue and that the seam is tight, then place weighted boards over the seams to keep them flat while the glue sets.

VARIATION: To close any gaps in loop-pile carpet seams, use a knee kicker to gently push the seam edges together on the tape while the adhesive is still hot.

13 Continue seaming the fill-in pieces together. Once the tape adhesive has dried, turn the seamed piece over and cut a fresh edge to be seamed with the large piece of carpet as done in step 8. Reheat and remove about 1½" of tape from the end of each seam to keep it from overlapping the tape on the large piece.

14 Use hot-glue seam tape to join the seamed fill-in pieces to the large piece of carpet, repeating steps 9 to 11.

15 If laying carpet in a closet, cut a fill-in piece and join it to the main carpet with hot-glue seam tape, using the same technique.

(continued next page)

How to Cut & Seam Carpet (continued)

TIP: At radiators, pipes, and other obstructions, cut slits in the carpet. First, cut long slits from the edge of the carpet to the obstruction, then cut short cross-slits where the carpet will fit around the obstruction.

TIP: To fit carpet around partition walls where the edges of the wall or door jamb meet the floor, make diagonal cuts from the edge of the carpet at the center of the wall to the points where the edges of the door jamb meet the floor.

How to Stretch & Secure Carpet

1 Before you start to stretch the seamed carpet, read through this entire section and create a stretching sequence similar to the one shown here. Start the process by fastening the carpet at a doorway threshold, using carpet transitions (pages 110 to 111).

2 If the doorway is close to a corner, use the knee kicker to secure the carpet to the tackless strips between the door and the corner. Also secure a few feet of carpet along the adjacent wall, again working toward the corner.

3 Use a power stretcher (page 109) to stretch carpet toward the wall opposite the door, bracing the tail block with a length of 2 × 4 placed across the door opening. Secure the carpet onto the tackless strips with a stair tool or the head of a hammer (inset).

Leaving the tail block in place and moving only the stretcher head, continue stretching and securing carpet along the wall, working toward the nearest corner in 12" to 24" increments.

4 With the power stretcher still extended from the doorway to the opposite side of the room, knee-kick the carpet onto the tackless strips along the closest wall, starting near the corner closest to the stretcher tail. Disengage and move the stretcher only if it gets in the way.

5 Reposition the stretcher so its tail block is against the center of the wall you just secured (step 4). Stretch and secure carpet along the opposite wall, working from the center toward a corner. NOTE: If there is a closet in an adjacent wall, work toward that wall, not the closet.

(continued next page)

How to Stretch & Secure Carpet (continued)

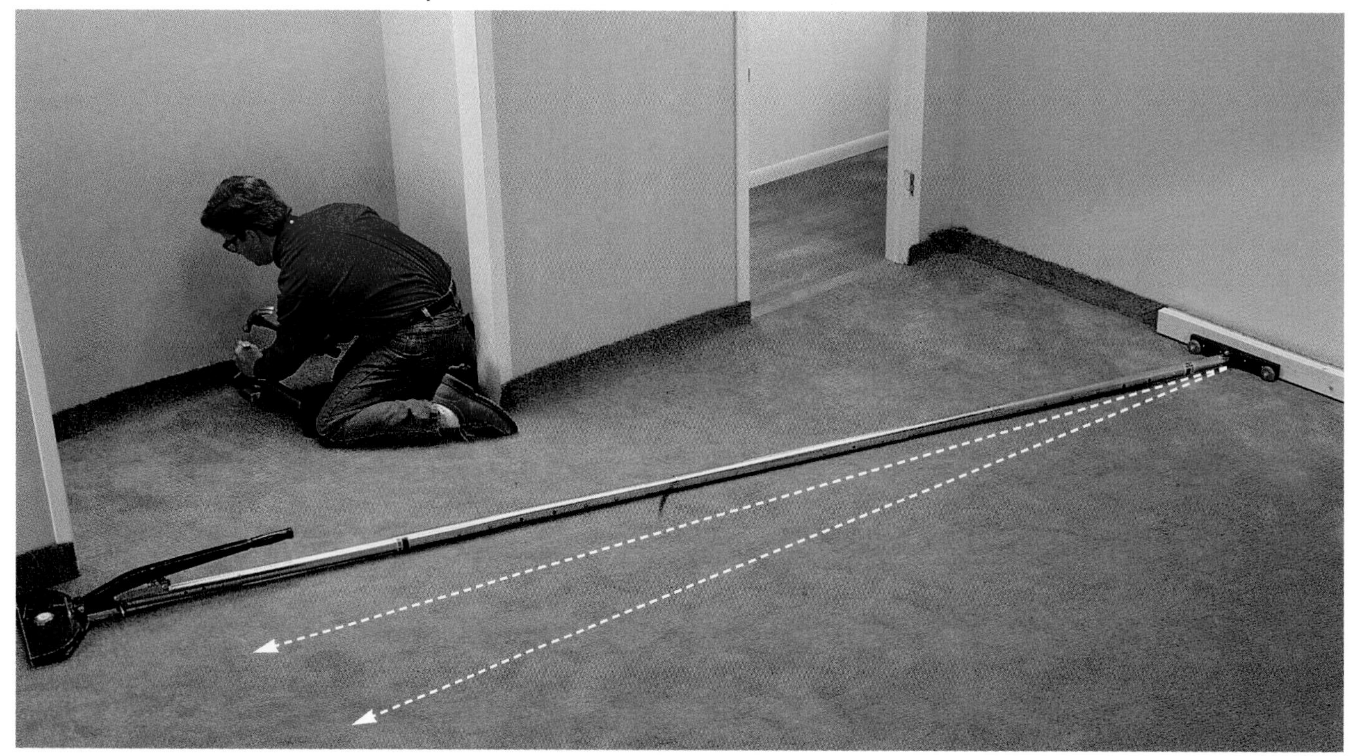

6 Use the knee-kicker to stretch and secure the carpet inside the closet (if any). Stretch and fasten the carpet against the back wall first, then do the side walls. After carpet in closet is stretched and secured, use the kicker to secure the carpet along the walls next to the closet. Disengage the power stretcher only if it gets in the way.

7 Return the head of the power stretcher to the center of the wall, then finish securing carpet along this wall, working toward the other corner of the room.

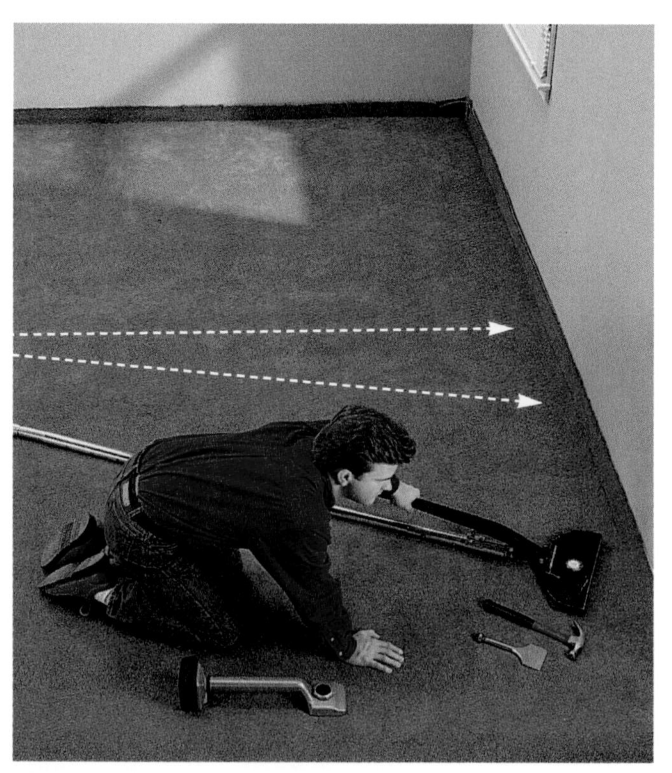

8 Reposition the stretcher to secure the carpet along the last wall of the room, working from the center toward the corners. The tail block should be braced against the opposite wall.

Tip: Locate any floor vents under the stretched carpet, then use a utility knife to carefully cut the carpet away, starting at the center. It is important that this be done after the stretching is completed.

9 Use a carpet edge trimmer to trim surplus carpet away from the walls. At corners, use a utility knife to finish the cuts.

10 Tuck the trimmed edges of the carpet neatly into the gaps between the tackless strips and the walls, using a stair tool and hammer.

Basic Techniques for Carpeting Stairs

Where practical, try to carpet stairs with a single strip of carpet. If you must use two or more pieces, plan the layout so the pieces meet where a riser meets a tread. Do not use seam tape to join pieces in the middle of a tread or riser.

The project shown here is a staircase that is enclosed on both sides. For open staircases, turn down the edges of the carpet and tack down with carpet tacks.

Everything You Need:

Tools: basic hand tools (page 27), stair tool, knee kicker.

Materials: Tackless strips, padding, carpet.

On stairways, tackless strips are attached about 1" above treads and about ¾" from risers. Where two or more pieces of carpet are needed, the pieces should meet at the back corner of a step, where a riser and tread meet (called the "crotch" of the stair).

How to Carpet Stairs

1 Measure the width of the stairway, then add together the vertical rise and horizontal run of the steps to determine how much carpet you will need. Use a straightedge and utility knife to carefully cut the carpet to the correct dimensions (page 115).

2 Fasten tackless strips to the risers and treads. On risers, the strips should be about 1" above the treads; on treads, about ¾" from the risers. Make sure the pins point toward the crotch. On the bottom riser, leave a gap equal to ⅔ the carpet thickness.

3 For each step, cut a piece of carpet padding the width of the stair and long enough to cover the tread and a few inches of the riser below it. Staple the padding in place.

4 Position the carpet on the stairs with the pile direction pointing down. Secure the bottom edge, using a stair tool to tuck the end of the carpet between the tackless strip and the floor.

5 Use a knee kicker and stair tool to stretch carpet onto the tackless strip on the first tread. Start in the center of the stair, then alternate kicks on either side until the carpet is completely secured in the stair.

6 Use a hammer and the stair tool to firmly wedge carpet into the back corner of the stair. Repeat this process for each stair.

7 Where two carpet pieces meet, secure the edge of the upper carpet piece first, then stretch and secure the lower piece.

INDEX

Product Information:

If you have difficulty finding any of the following materials featured in this book, call the manufacturers and ask for the name of the nearest sales representatives. The representatives can direct you to local retailers that stock these useful products.

Anso® nylon carpet (page 14 top)
AlliedSignal Fibers
2100 Fiber Park Drive
Dalton, GA 30720

Crack-isolation membrane (page 49)
Dal-guard™, Dallas Specialty
1-800-222-5644

DuPont approved *Stainmaster*® carpet (page 14 bottom, page 15, page 21 bottom left)
1-717-291-1491

Embossing leveler (page 34)
Color Tile, Inc.
1-800-688-8063

Thresholds and reducers for hardwood floors, including T-shaped thresholds (page 92)
Bruce Hardwood Floors
1-800-529-5903

Creative Publishing International, Inc. offers a variety of how-to books.
For information write:
Creative Publishing International, Inc.
Subscriber Books
5900 Green Oak Drive
Minnetonka, MN 55343